They Said I Co
But I Did!

EVELYN B. ECHOLS

AMP&RSAND, INC.

Chicago, Illinois

13 12 11 10   5 4 3 2

ISBN 978-0-9818126-1-8

www.evelynechols.com

Cover photo:
Jennifer Girard

Book Design:
David Robson, Robson Design

Published by:
Ampersand, Inc.
1050 N. State Street, Chicago, IL 60610
www.ampersandworks.com

Printed in the United States of America

To the Echols Brigadiers

*A group of 50 successful Chicago businesswomen
with whom I have spent many hours
of fun and laughter*

ACKNOWLEDGMENTS

To the many devoted family members and friends
who have supported me through both good times and bad...
with special thanks to

The O'Neill/Conley families
John Meinert
Virginia Rogers
Ron Tully
The Little Sisters of the Poor

And deepest gratitude to
Helen Gurley Brown and
Walter Cronkite
who encouraged me
to write this book

CONTENTS

Dedication..3

Acknowledgments...5

Preface...9

Introduction.. 11

1. *My Childhood Years* 12

2. *Tragic Lessons of the Depression Years* 21

3. *My Miraculous Introduction to New York City* 28

4. *My Travel Career in the Midst of World War II*.......... 34

5. *David Enters my Life* 39

6. *Life in Venezuela* 43

7. *I Become an Entrepreneur and Joan Crawford*
   Contributes Greatly to my Success............................ 54

8. *Our Happy Move to Chicago*................................. 65

9. *Cast Thy Bread upon the Water* 75

10. *My New Entrepreneurial Adventure* 85

11. *Life Takes a Turn* 88

12. *God, Why Are You Leaning on me So Heavily?* 94

13. *A New Career Emerges at Age 80* 97

14. *Life Continues to Be a Challenge*........................... 100

15. *My Three Favorite Trips*....................................... 103

PREFACE

Dear Reader:

As you read this book, I hope you will embark on your own journey of self-discovery. Begin keeping a daily record of the events you are experiencing. As you go forward, these notes will guide you through the trials, tribulations and victories that you surely will find in your future. I wish you peace, serenity and a triumphant, long and happy life.

Evelyn B. Echols
Chicago, Illinois
January 2009

INTRODUCTION

As I approach age 94, I realize every day how right I was in my early years to keep copious notes on the current happenings in my world. There is no doubt that every event in your life, good or bad, if handled calmly and thoughtfully, will make your future brighter. For example, during the Great Depression I learned how to do without, making it possible for me to react with equilibrium when, at age 80, I experienced one disaster after another.

An adage I agree with totally is this: prior to every hour of work, spend at least five hours in contemplative dialogue with yourself. In this time of turmoil, when there is such instability in our lives, I believe that it is urgent for us to take the time to concentrate on what we can do to enhance our future.

That is why I have written this book.

CHAPTER 1

My Childhood Years

On a farm, everyone has chores and obligations. My father told me early on that unless I took great care of my animals, I would not be allowed to keep them. That is the first lesson I can remember learning and this sense of responsibility made a real contribution to my later success.

Being born and raised on a farm was, without a doubt, one of the blessings in my life. Difficult, yes, but being able to roam free and to experience the incredible joy that Mother Nature affords us taught me that if we take the time to study and appreciate the natural world, our lives will overflow with beauty.

From my earliest years I was privileged to have a wide array of pet animals. Since I was an only child until age 12, my pets were a great comfort to me. My beautiful duck, Harry, followed me throughout the day. When I began school, he sat by the gate and waited for me. When he saw me, he would flap his wings and quack wildly. My sassy pig, Sarah; my goat, Tallulah, who could jump any fence on the farm; my gentle, loving sheep, Samantha; and my faithful dog, Spot, were also beloved pets, but Harry was special. One of my saddest memories from those early years happened the morning I went out to open Harry's little pad. I was not getting my usual noisy greeting. The door was partially opened and when I looked in, to my horror, there were just a few white feathers. A fox had gotten in during the night and I had no more Harry. My heart was broken.

When I began school at the age of five, I received a gift that is every child's dream – my very own pony. His name was Socks, since he was black with four white feet. As many Shetland ponies are, he was unpredictable. I would ride him the two miles to school, tie his bridle to the saddle and he would happily trot home. In the afternoon, my parents saddled him up and he would come get me at school. However, if he was in one of his more fractious moods, we would be riding along peacefully and then he would suddenly rise up on his back feet, toss me off, and leave me to walk home. He did this frequently when the weather was cold or rainy, which prompted me to learn to curse like a sailor at an early age. It was only at my father's insistence that I fed this culprit. The impudent look he gave me as I entered the barn would infuriate me even more!

My one-room school had a magnificent and dedicated teacher, Mary Migglio. She taught 20 children in grades one through eight. Miss Migglio would arrive at school very early in the winter months and by the time we got there, she would have the potbelly stove burning brightly and would serve us hot chocolate and cookies. We learned so much from Miss Migglio. One advantage was that while she was conducting classes for the upper grades, we could listen and absorb more than one would think possible. Today, while others are busily getting their calculators to answer a mathematical problem, I usually come up with the solution much more quickly. For this I thank Mary Migglio, who gave me my greatest educational experience and one from which I still benefit.

At an early age, I had another experience that has influenced me to this day. When my father married my mother, he built a house next to my grandparents'. But it contained only one bedroom, and since my grandparents lived in a big, beautiful, historic house that had been built by my great-grandparents when they arrived from England around 1850, I was invited to live with them.

Great grandfather, Brazilla Bassett, wrote to his family back in England that in order to see over the Illinois prairie grass he had to stand on his horse! His wife, Lucinda, must have been quite a pioneer, too. She was 37 when they arrived at Tonica and delivered five children with the help of an Iroquois squaw in the following years. It still amazes me that four of the five children attended the University

Our family home near Tonica, Illinois built in 1870 by my great-great grandfather, Brazilla Bassett. I am standing on the running board, waiting for my grandparents to take me for a ride.

of Illinois. Irene became a teacher of English at the Sorbonne in Paris. Ada became a missionary in China. Arthur became a famous concert pianist. Herbert became a professor at Macomb University and Ira, thank goodness for me, decided to stay on the farm.

It was a memorable day when I packed up my assortment of rag dolls and moved to my grandparents' house next door. I was delighted to find that Grandma had assigned me a beautiful bedroom/living room on the second floor. I was enchanted by this luxurious windfall, since at my parents' home I had been sleeping on a daybed in the living room and had little space for my belongings. Here I had a feather bed with a brass headboard covered with a gaily decorated quilt, which had been made by my grandmother. I had my very own dresser and a fairly large closet. The bedroom opened into a lovely sitting area, which was furnished with two easy chairs, an antique desk, and a commode, which contained a wonderful pink and white china basin and pitcher. On the floor was a bright red, green and blue Indian rug, and at the windows were white organza tied-back curtains.

Another joy was a door leading to the porch rooftop, which was surrounded by tall oak trees. On warm nights my dog, Spot, and I often slept outside. When my eyes became acclimated to the wonder of the night, I could see millions of stars moving through the skies and was oh so enchanted when I saw several of them fall during the course of the night. Night sounds in the country were wonderful, especially when a gentle breeze kept the tree leaves making music as they moved to and fro. I loved the sound of the baby birds chirping, an occasional moo coming from the barn, the sad wail of a coyote, and the early morning crow of the roosters as the sun came up.

I was nurtured by two quite different cultures. My father's family was very strict English Methodist and my mother's very large family was gregarious, witty Irish Catholic. In my grandfather and grandmother Bassett's home, all was in order and my grandmother's beautiful gardens made this an extraordinary place of peace and serenity. In my grandmother and grandfather Coleman's home, the opposite was true. This was a home always in complete turmoil. We joined 20–25 people there every Sunday for lunch. There were the immediate Coleman family, plus cousins, nieces and nephews. The extremely long dining table was covered with a beautiful, white Irish linen table cloth. Relatives were asked to bring their own linen napkins on which they had printed their initials in ink. My cousin, Buddy, and I hated these interminable meals and whenever possible we would sneak into the pantry, grab the ingredients for lunch and dash down a very steep hill to a place where a wonderful creek ran through the property. After removing our shoes and socks, we would wade in the cool water and then sit under the willow trees, thoroughly enjoying ourselves, paying no attention whatsoever to the demanding calls for us to come to lunch.

Actually, I enjoyed a closer relationship with my father's family than with my mother's, no doubt stemming from the fact that I lived with my grandparents and the fact that my grandmother Bassett – a stately, beautiful, hardworking, lovely lady – was the number one person in my life. Grandmother Bassett was my guardian angel. As a matter of fact I would never have had the pleasure of having my mother with me had it not been for Grandma Bassett's medicinal skills.

I was an only child until age 12, when my brother Coleman was born, followed by the birth of Kenneth, Robert and my sister, Gloria. I was already away at boarding school by the time Coleman arrived, so I spent very little time with my siblings. It was only in later years that we truly got to know one another.

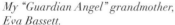

My "Guardian Angel" grandmother,   *My grandfather, Ira Bassett.*
Eva Bassett.

On the day I was born, April 5, 1915, the doctor had spent the
night at our house, caring for my mother who had developed uremic
poisoning, which in those days was usually fatal. In the morning he
advised the family that my mother was dying and there was nothing
more that he could do. Grandma Bassett arrived shortly thereafter
carrying a huge tub and many wool blankets. She asked that the
blankets be submerged in the tub of boiling water and that one be
brought to her quickly, every 15 minutes. She wrapped my mother
in these blankets and after one full day, Grandma's remedy had succeeded in perspiring the poison from my mother's pores. Her temperature began to subside. Needless to say, the doctor was in shock
when he came to the house the following day, expecting to sign my
mother's death certificate. He found her sitting up in bed, joyfully
holding her new baby.

I ran to Grandma with all problems great or small, and she always
had a remedy. As a result, up to the age of 16, I had only visited a
doctor's office twice. Grandma's home cures, many of which I still
use today, were miraculous. For example, if I showed the slightest
sniffle, Grandma would rub a horrible mixture of turpentine and
lard on my chest and cover it with flannel. (Later, Vicks Vapor Rub
was substituted for this remedy.) She would also keep me supplied
with several pitchers of orange juice and water and I was not allowed

Our family in 1929. Dad (Frank) with Coleman, and Mom (Irene) with Kenneth and me at the age of 14. Robert and Gloria would come along later.

out of bed. And of course this meant that some poor chicken would lose its life, because she was sure I would never recuperate without chicken soup.

In those days I was sometimes subject to what we know today as a migraine headache. Grandma's remedy there was a darkened room, ice packs and one drop of iodine in a glass of cold water for nausea, which usually accompanied my headaches. I was totally amazed years later when a very renowned doctor in New York recommended the same remedy.

Grandma was not only my physician without a license. Many of the neighbors depended on her resources, too. For example, if someone had a broken arm or leg, they would come to Grandma and she would immediately go down to the cellar and bring up a large glass of her homemade dandelion wine. After the patient had finished drinking this concoction she would then suddenly grasp the broken limb and give it a quick jerk, which usually generated a holler that could be heard from some distance. She would then apply one of her homemade splints and send her patient home to bed.

Grandma was the one person everyone trusted to pick wild herbs, which she then cooked and administered to us as a cure for stomach disorders. She also could distinguish a toadstool from a mushroom.

She was a great believer in garlic and always said that it was a natural antibiotic, although she did not use that term in those days. As a result I believe it is thanks to my garlic intake that I have been able to stay healthy without the use of antibiotics. At age 94 and counting, I know without question that my dependence on Grandma's cure-alls is responsible for the fact that I have been able to survive this long life with a minimal amount of medication and infrequent visits to the doctor's office. My doctor probably sees me once a year.

Grandma thoroughly believed that as the seasons changed, the body needed a cleansing and time to adjust, too. So out came the bottle of castor oil and no matter how she tried to camouflage this unpleasant dosage with orange juice, it still was never palatable. Everyone was advised that while the body was adjusting to a new climate, one needed more rest. So, we all spent a good deal more time in bed during these periods.

I loved winter, when the snow was so deep that no one could leave the house until a path to the barns and the outdoor john had been shoveled. During such a snow, it seemed as if the Earth stood still, complete silence. This was a time when we were isolated from the rest of the world. The family gathered together, read books, played cards, ate the delicious meals that my mother prepared, especially her freshly baked angel food cake, pies and cookies.

In those days there was no television, no video games. The only entertainment was a gramophone with a huge speaker. On occasion, my grandfather would allow us to play his collection of John Phillip Souza recordings. After a long winter, how excited we were to see the first signs of spring, when someone would sight a jonquil.

Spring was always my favorite season, because summer was often very hot, even though our numerous trees afforded us an ongoing breeze throughout the warmest days. Summer of course, despite the heat, was a particularly carefree time. My great aunts and uncles came to the farm for a sabbatical every summer. After dinner, they would gather on the spacious porch and, as I sat quietly in a corner, they would mesmerize me with conversations about their incredible experiences over the past year. I learned to listen very closely and believe that these evenings were primarily responsible for my early interest in travel and later the travel business.

When fall came along I especially enjoyed the harvest when our neighbors would arrive to help my father reap the crops, transferring some to our barns and the balance to market. The wives would be there to help prepare a gigantic lunch for this hungry group. The huge luncheons would include fried or roasted chickens prepared in large vats, salads and dozens of desserts, including cakes, pies, brownies and cookies. My friend, Agnes, and I had the responsibility of keeping the workers supplied with water and lemonade. We would ride our ponies from field to field and have a very merry time. It was pretty exciting to watch the horse drawn reapers and the entire process of harvesting the crops.

One of the fall events I looked forward to the most was set off by phones ringing as neighbors called one another advising the arrival of the gypsies. I have no idea where they came from or where they were going, but they were scouring our area, living on what they could steal. Word spread quickly when they were in our neighborhood. I was not allowed to go outdoors when they were present because my parents were afraid that they would kidnap me. However, I found them to be wildly exciting.

They came by in covered wagons, their attire a beautiful array of bright colors. They seemed to be the only happy people around. I recall one day when my grandmother grabbed her broom and rushed out to chase a young woman who was filling her basket with apples from our orchard. She was spectacularly beautiful, wearing a bright green, off-the-shoulder blouse, and a floor-length multicolored skirt. She was in the direct light of a very bright sun. Her shiny black hair and her statuesque posture made her a vision to behold. My grandmother's angry demands that she "drop the apples and get out of here" fazed her not one iota. Only when her basket was full did she start walking slowly toward the road, turning back insolently to thank my grandmother for her kindness. Stealing pigs and chickens seemed to be their night activity, while innocently stealing fruits and vegetables from gardens and orchards was a day activity.

My father and the other men in the neighborhood were not so enchanted and they never dared go to bed until the gypsies had left the area. My father napped on the sofa in the living room with his shotgun nearby and when he heard a great commotion in the chicken house or the barn doors opening, he would go out and fire skyward to frighten the marauders away.

I was particularly happy when the gypsies came by late in the afternoon because this meant they would probably set up camp within a mile of our place. If I kept my bedroom window open, I could see their campfire glowing brightly and listen to the beautiful melodies being played on what was probably a zither or possibly a guitar. I would visualize their singing and dancing to this melodic, romantic music and imagined myself living as a gypsy. It seemed like such a wonderful life!

LESSONS LEARNED

Some of the lessons I learned in my early years made an indelible impression on me. For example, my love of nature and animals took root at that time and I still endeavor to support any effort to protect these two great blessings which contribute so much to our well being and happiness.

Another lessoned learned was the importance of being able to appreciate your own company and spend time alone. This is an invaluable gift.

However, the greatest lesson I learned during this time was my grandmother's home remedies, which I know without a doubt, are responsible in great part to the good health I enjoy. Garlic is my only and most effective antibiotic.

CHAPTER 2

Tragic Lessons
of the Depression Years

Being an only child for the first 12 years of my life and having only one girlfriend within a mile-and-a-half was at times very lonely. Therefore my friendship with Agnes Baldwin was very important to me. Agnes and I had become close friends from the time we began attending school.

She had her pony, Hubert, and I had Socks. We would ride our ponies to school, and during the summer, spent many days roaming the countryside at will. But our happy days on horseback soon came to an end during the Depression.

We often attended the auctions when banks were foreclosing on the farms of our friends and neighbors and offered whatever consolation we could to these poor, desperate families. Their land and all of their world possessions were sold for sometimes as little as a few thousand dollars. The auction that stands out in my memory was the dreadful day of Agnes's family bankruptcy sale.

On this particular say, I noticed that the auctioneer was as ill clad as some of the assembly. As he began asking for bids, I felt that he had been doing this for so long that he was completely desensitized and seemed unaware of the tragedy he was initiating. As I observed those around me, the despair was far worse than at any funeral I had ever attended. The families – some stoic and other with tears streaming down their faces, hopeless expressions of the spectators, many wondering if they would be next – and the rundown house, barn and machinery sheds in the background, just like an Andrew Wyeth painting. The memory of that remains with me today.

Suddenly Agnes ran out sobbing hysterically. She threw her arms around her pony's neck and would not let it go. Her father finally had to convince her that she had to release Hubert. The auctioneer had sold the pony for $7 and none of Agnes's friends could afford to outbid the miserable, thoughtless creature who was taking the pony from her. As the truck pulled out of the yard, the only sound that could be heard was Agnes screaming as family and friends tried to console her. This proved to be the most frightening experience of my life. Not only was I devastated by what I just witnessed, but I was also wondering how long it would be before I might lose Socks under the same circumstances. When leaving the auction, I mentioned this to my father and he replied in a quivering voice, "Evelyn, I cannot guarantee that this will not happen. I'm doing the very best I can."

Things seemed to go from bad to worse. My father no longer had regular hired men working on the farm. My mother and father seemed to have no time at all for rest and relaxation. By the summer of 1930, many men were walking through the countryside begging for a day's work. My parents never turned anyone away. Proud men who had worked their entire lives and had been self-supporting were now walking up and down country roads, offering to work a full day for a meal and permission to sleep in our farm.

One day as I was leaving school, I passed the St. Patrick's Church breadline where desperate people were lined up to get a cup of coffee and a slice of bread. I could not believe it when I saw Henry, the man who had repaired our shoes for my entire life, standing in this line. When he saw me, he began to cry. When I arrived home from school, I immediately told my parents about it and my father instantly harnessed up a horse and buggy while my mother prepared a package of different cheeses, eggs, milk, other farm products and a huge slice of her favorite angel food cake to take to Henry. Our family then kept him supplied with adequate food until 1933 when he was able to get work again.

In 1933, President Roosevelt and Congress ordered the banks closed and put an end to the bankruptcy sales. Congress then passed the Work Progress Administration, which hired more than eight million people in the following years. Most of this work was in construction. Some built roads, dams and bridges. Another two million people were employed in the Civilian Conversation Corps, taking care of government parks, planting trees, and fighting forest fires. Although some felt this was a waste of government money, the President saw it as a better solution than handing out welfare checks.

As the economy improved in the following years, everyone's spirits began to brighten. In celebration, our neighbors got together, cleaned out our barn, and held the first barn dance we had had in several years. A keg of beer and soft drinks were provided as fiddlers played for happy survivors who danced the night away. The economy picked up and many were able to repurchase their farms and life resumed in America, but of course, at a terrible price. Many of the fathers, husbands and sons who were expected to come home to the family farms, did not return, and others came back so physically or mentally disabled that they could never reclaim their lives prior to 1929.

However, I thought that nothing could compare to my despair shortly after I began dating at age 17. My first date was an attractive young man, a football player at LaSalle-Peru High School. We met at the counter of our ice cream parlor, where many of us gathered after school. I was thrilled beyond words when he invited me to go with him to a hot dog roast on the following Saturday night. I wore my relatively new Easter suit that evening. I had a wonderful time and since I had developed quite a crush on Steve, I was enchanted when he invited me to a movie later in the week. Since the suit was my only dressy garment, I added a colorful scarf to it. I even made a blouse from a piece of fabric I had found in the attic. Steve drove into the yard and when I ran out to meet him, he said to me, "Is that all the clothes you have?" I had not yet gotten into the car, but when I said, "Yes, it is," he turned on the engine and drove off without saying another word. I was not only devastated, but also totally humiliated. The only good thing that came from that ghastly experience was that I lost 10 pounds in the subsequent weeks because I had completely lost my appetite. I made up my mind at that time that this would never happen to me again. So, as soon as I began earning money, I invested more of it in my wardrobe and became something of a clotheshorse.

At the time, the Ku Klux Klan was quite prominent in our area. I remember one great adventure when my friends and I hid out in the bushes near our neighbor's farm and watched the ceremonial cross burning, trying to identify our neighbors under their sheets and masks. These people were our neighbors; I had no fear of them, even though we knew that the Klan hated Roman Catholics.

In thinking back, why were the Ku Klux Klan so prominent in our area? There were very few Catholics in our neighborhood, no Jews and no other minorities, so who was there to hate? I still can't understand it because the people I knew all throughout my childhood were loving, kind and helpful. We were good friends. What were they afraid of?

As you can see, LaSalle County was a very interesting community. Between the gypsies and the Ku Klux Klan, there was also the world famous Chicago gangster Al Capone. Those were the years that Al Capone and his gang were running beer from Chicago to Peoria. Their route took them right through LaSalle County. It was a wide-open town, where gambling was allowed. Capone's gang supplied the beer sold in the local taverns. The reality of the gang wars was brought home to us one Sunday morning. My father, who was not a churchgoer, would drop off my mother and me at the Roman Catholic Church and wait for us at a nearby tavern. One day after mass, we went to the tavern to meet him and found a large crowd gathered. The tavern owner, who had been buying his beer from another supplier, had had a visit from Capone's men the night before. They had shot up his entire back glass bar, except the area where the owner had been standing at the time. Not surprisingly, he changed beer distributors.

At about that time I had transferred to high school in Ottawa, Illinois, where there were about a dozen other boarders. This was even worse than the school I had previously attended because I couldn't go home on the weekends. My last two years in high school were equally depressing. They were spent at Josephinum Academy in Chicago which my Aunt had previously attended. Now I was completely miserable because I was only permitted to go home for Christmas and Easter week. Because of my unhappiness I was not a good student and I'm sure the good sisters were as glad to see me leave as I was to go.

I went home from Josephinum to a most difficult situation. My mother was suffering from a hip problem and could barely walk. But the poor woman had four children to care for. Shortly after I returned from school, she was operated on, but at that time, hip replacement surgery was unknown and the pain from the surgery only made her condition worse. Money was tight, and because of my mother's problem, I had the enormous responsibility of taking care of my siblings, cooking, and doing the laundry.

In those years, a woman's choice of career was either teaching or nursing, so I opted to pursue nursing at St. Mary's Hospital in nearby LaSalle. At that time it consisted of on-the-job training with little formal course work. After six weeks at St. Mary's Hospital, I was already scrubbing up in surgery. We were on the floor from 7:00 A.M. to 7:00 P.M. with two, one hour rest breaks during the day. We worked six-and-a-half days a week and were on call for emergencies at night. We had two Sunday afternoons off per month.

One snowy night, a friend and I decided that we needed a break from the monotony, and so we made a date with two interns. The plan called for me to sneak past the supervisor's desk, wearing my uniform. I'd wait under my friend's window and she would throw down our dress clothes. She'd then sneak out and join me outside. We had already made arrangements to change clothes at a friend's house. What we had not planned on was the dozens of utility wires under my friend's window. When she threw the garments down to me, about half of them got caught in the wiring. Despondent, I snuck back into our quarters. The next morning, the supervisor announced the mysterious arrival of a number of garments on the wires outside her window and said that they would stay there until someone claimed them. We had to choose between losing our clothes or losing our Sunday afternoons off for the foreseeable future. We kept quiet. I lost my winter coat, which I could not afford to replace, and she lost her only good dress. The supervisor let them wave in the breeze for a week. Each time we passed her window, we were reminded of our folly.

After I completed two years of nurse's training, I went down to St. Louis, where my mother's sister, Genevieve, a Catholic nun, was an executive at the Catholic hospital there. This was quite an experience because I had left home with only enough money to see me through for two or three days. When I arrived at the hospital, I was met with unhappy news that Sister Genevieve was on retreat in Kentucky and would not return for several days. In the meantime, no one showed great interest in hiring me.

In desperation, I rented a small room in a boarding house very near the hospital. By the third day, despite my frugal food budget, I ran out of money. I didn't want to stress my parents, so for the first time in my life, I actually went without food for two days. I have no idea how my very nice landlady discovered that I was not eating, but when she brought me a plate of cold cuts and potato salad, I was so grateful in thanking her, that I broke down crying. She very kindly invited me to breakfast the next day and I was so ravenously hungry that I ate practically everything in sight.

When Sister Genevieve arrived home, I was immediately employed. When they asked me when I'd like to start, I said I'd be back in an hour with my uniform. This would enable me to be there in time for lunch.

I spent only a short time in St. Louis since an opportunity came up for me to accompany a gentleman who was diagnosed with tuber-culosis to the Jewish National Tuberculosis Hospital in Denver. I jumped at the opportunity to see the Great West. On arriving there, I accepted a position, but shortly thereafter, I was again on the move.

I had always dreamed of visiting New York. From what I had gleaned from magazines and newspapers, this city seemed to me to epitomize everything that was glamorous and exciting. In April 1936, my friend, Helen, and I saved up enough money for a trip to New York by car shuttle – the cheapest way we could get there. I wish I could say that I had wonderful memories of my trip east. But with our luggage crammed into the back seat and driving straight through the night, it was extremely uncomfortable. By the time we entered the Holland Tunnel, we were loopy with fatigue and barely noticed that we'd arrived in the Big Apple.

LESSONS LEARNED

———

The Great Depression was a harsh teacher.
The tragedy of abject poverty taught me compassion for those
who were less fortunate. I learned during this time
how to do without and to appreciate the blessings we still enjoy.

My years in boarding school and nurse training were most difficult,
but they made it possible for me to obtain a job
in New York in 1936 at the height of the Depression.
All of this put me in great stead, when at age 80 I once again
fell on bad times and had to alter dramatically the affluent life
I had been leading for many years.

———

CHAPTER 3

My Miraculous Introduction to New York City

elen and I arrived in New York City on my 21st birthday for what was to be a one-week vacation. It turned into 26 wonderful years in this incredible city! After our long ride, Helen and I got ourselves a hotel room on 63rd and Broadway and slept for almost one entire day.

We then decided to take our first adventurous walk down to the world renowned 42nd and Broadway and what a glorious revelation this proved to be. We were mesmerized by the sights and sounds of this incredible street.

In my excitement, I turned to Helen, hugged her and said, "I'm never leaving here." What made me think that I would be able to get a job in this highly competitive market when I had absolutely no experience and we were in the heart of the Depression? It must have been my utter trust that God would provide.

But if I were going to stay, I needed to find work immediately. Fortunately, the desk clerk at our hotel very kindly gave me a copy of the Want Ads section of the Sunday *New York Times* and sure enough, there was a job in a private maternity hospital in an ideal location, at

56th and Lexington. The hospital's owner was an Italian doctor who called each mother-to-be "Rosie." Who Rosie was, I never knew, but her name was shouted up and down the hospital corridors all day, like a delightful mantra: "Push, Rosie, push!"

Someone asked me recently what motivated me to keep on moving. My response was, "I grew up during the Great Depression and learned early in life that if you didn't work, you didn't eat. I love to eat!"

One of the most fortunate things that happened to me occurred when I moved into the Barbizon Hotel for Women. This was where almost every unmarried woman who came to New York in the 1930s resided. It was a safe haven in the big city. In later years I discovered Grace Kelly had lived there when she first came to New York and had shared a room with Donna Atwater, who became one of my very dearest friends when I later moved to Chicago.

Not surprisingly, men hung around the Barbizon Hotel entrance like vultures, 24 hours a day.

Several of the famous, most glamorous models living in the Barbizon Hotel took me under their wings. They were fun, unpretentious working girls with outrageous names: Dulcet Tone, Choo Choo Johnson, Dorian Lee (who later owned a highly successful modeling agency in Paris) and Honey Child Wilder. They'd been in Manhattan long enough to know the ropes. Choo Choo was probably the most beautiful woman I had ever met and a wonderful friend. She had a delightful sense of humor.

Lucky for me, these kind, worldly girls decided that I needed a complete makeover if I wanted to survive in the big city. They accompanied me to 7th Avenue to stock up my tiny wardrobe at wholesale prices and then to their hair stylists, who took a dim view of my unprofessional hairstyle and makeup. I now felt transformed – an Alice in Wonderland.

One day, Dulcet and several other models invited me out to a movie. On the way, they stopped by the John Powers Modeling Agency to pick up their assignment. As I was waiting for them in the reception area, a gentleman walked by and glanced at me. He stopped, turned around and looked at me intently. He asked me whom I was waiting to see, introducing himself as John Powers. I was flabbergasted when he invited me into his office. Smiling, he told me, "You're the most typical Midwesterner I've seen in a long,

long time. I think you'd be ideal if you want to model for the Montgomery Ward catalogue." And here I thought I was the personification of New York. They took photographs, and I did, in fact, do a good deal of work for the catalogue, but I soon realized that I'd never make it as a top model.

My new glamorous friends began inviting me to accompany them to some very elegant parties and I soon realized that I was not knowledgeable enough to carry on an intelligent conversation with these New York sophis-

Early days in New York where I was spotted as a "typical mid-westerner."

ticates. I further knew that I had to be able to converse in topics that were covered in *The New York Times*, *Women's Wear Daily*, *The Wall Street Journal* and the *New Yorker* magazine. Therefore, I spent a good deal of my leisure time reading.

The next problem that I encountered was that I knew absolutely nothing about art or classical music. Fortunately I am a very quick learner. I spent many weekends visiting the Metropolitan Museum where I sat in on lectures and took advantage of any cultural events that were advertised in the media.

I would call my parents and tell them that I would be staying for a few more months and when those months passed, I would call again and say that I would stay for a few more months, to the point where they got accustomed to the idea that I was now a New York resident. I visited them periodically.

By this time I was dating one of the Ellis brothers, Jack, who was a sales manager for RKO pictures. We eventually married in September of 1939. Jack added many dimensions to my education. As I accompanied him to motion picture premieres and social events in the motion picture industry, another new world was opening for me. Jack also taught me an appreciation for the opera and theater, which was of course, a very broadening, exciting experience. Gradually I became more worldly-wise than I had been when I arrived in Manhattan.

At the time, Joseph P. Kennedy was president of RKO pictures. I remember one evening at a dinner dance. He and the glamorous movie star, Gloria Swanson, his long time lady love, were out on the dance floor and as he passed us, he said, "Jack, that's a pretty girl you've got on your arm!" He would say the same thing every time we met and Gloria, at that point, would give me a cold smile, showing her enormous teeth and dance him away.

Jack was a man of many gifts, including real talent as a song lyricist. At one time, he was working with Fred Astaire on a number – a venture that allowed me to meet this delightful, charming man on several occasions. The things that struck me the most about this gentleman was his graciousness and his modesty. If Jack and he were troubled about a lyric, Fred would always defer to Jack, even though I thought Fred's suggestions were usually the better of the two. I was fascinated by the elegance of Fred's wardrobe and went out shopping for new shirts and ties for Jack after our first meeting.

Carmen Lombardo, Guy's brother, also worked with Jack, and so we spent many Saturday evenings at the Roosevelt Hotel, where Guy Lombardo's orchestra played for many years. At the time, this was one of the most popular ballrooms in Manhattan. Long before I danced the night away there, I had listened to the broadcast, "Guy Lombardo and his Royal Canadians coming to you from the beautiful Roosevelt Hotel in New York." My dreams of the past years were coming to life.

Jack also co-wrote songs with Arthur Gershwin, George and Ira's younger brother. Arthur lived with his mother, Rose, in upper Manhattan. I was enthralled when we first visited Rose's apartment, with its view of Central Park, its elaborate furnishings, and wonderful collection of art. A beautiful grand piano stood in the living room. I loved going to her apartment when Jack and Arthur were working together, because George and Ira might be there. They visited their mother often when they were on the East Coast.

Rose was a marvelous character. She loved to play poker and quite often, while Jack and Arthur were busy composing, I would watch the poker game. Many of New York's most illustrious celebrities participated in these frays, including Oscar Levant. One of the most remarkable evenings of my life occurred when George had tired of gaming, went to the piano and invited me to sit with him as he played some of his more recent show tunes. I was amazed to see him improvise as he continued to play. I couldn't believe I was sharing a piano bench with one of my idols, George Gershwin.

Rose had taken an apparent liking to me and would often call and ask me to join her when she was going shopping. Her favorite designer at the time was Hattie Carnegie. She loved hats and wore them well. She was extremely parsimonious. For example, after a long night of playing poker, she would suggest that we all drive out to Ben Marden's, a noted casino in New Jersey. After losing hundreds of dollars gambling, she would not

The great cabaret singer, Julie Wilson, became one of my closest and dearest friends.

moan and groan about the money, but about the 25 cent toll on the George Washington Bridge. I found her most amusing and enjoyed many good times with her. However, George's death was an incredible tragedy for Rose and from that time on, she was not the jolly, garrulous person we had known.

Jack and I were now dating steadily. Jack loved the nightlife, and I have wonderful memories of evenings at El Morocco, where Howard Hughes usually sat with the owner, John Perona, and a bevy of beautiful women at the round table. Our favorite haunts were the Stork Club, where Sherman Billingsley, the owner, gave his favorite guests lovely scarves and perfume. We also enjoyed the Copacabana, with its famous cabaret entertainers, and the 21 Club, probably the most famous restaurant in the United States.

One of my most valued experiences occurred at the Copacabana in the early '40s where I was introduced to the now famous Julie Wilson, who was then dancing in the chorus at the Copa. I'm so grateful that today, Julie Wilson still remains one of my dearest friends.

LESSON LEARNED

———

New York, New York.
If you can make it there, you can make it anywhere.
And I Did!!!

Few people are as fortunate as I was in making the transition
from an unsophisticated farm girl to the glamorous life
I led in those early years. I quickly learned that if I were to truly
succeed in New York, it would be necessary for me to become
knowledgeable and able to converse about the arts
and the current events which were affecting our lives.

———

CHAPTER 4

My Travel Career in the Midst of World War II

In September of 1939, when Jack and I married, I quit my job at the hospital. Early on we discovered, to our grief, that we could not have children, so I decided to seek a position in the travel industry, since this had always been my goal.

I answered an ad for a position at Grant Advertising, the second largest international ad agency in the United States. The job at Grant's New York offices involved handling travel arrangements for agency executives. A charming woman, Kathi Norris, interviewed me. (She later became the mother of Koo Stark, the porn star and highly published girlfriend of England's Prince Andrew.) Kathi hired me immediately, and I began what would turn into a travel career that would last my entire life.

Sunday, December 7, 1941 was a bright sunny day in New York City. We had finished lunch and were now enjoying a quiet afternoon, reading *The New York Times* and listening to the broadcast of the New York Giants baseball game. Suddenly the broadcast was interrupted by an announcement that all service men and women must return to their stations immediately. There was no further information as to why, but obviously this was a very serious problem. We sat apprehensively listening for further word and when it was finally announced that Japan had attacked Pearl Harbor and we were now at war with Japan, we were in total disbelief and shock. Further announcements advised us to cover our windows and not allow any light to escape. We were also asked not to use the phone because the government needed all lines. We turned off all the lights, and when we looked outside in the direction of Times Square it seemed impossible that there was not one speck of light showing in the entire city. Jack and I decided to take a walk around the block. The only visible light came from the moon. The street was crowded with people and what an amazing surprise it was to see New Yorkers conversing with strangers. Everyone was frightened and apprehensive, especially those who had relatives in Hawaii or on the West Coast, where another strike was anticipated. We stayed very close to the radio that evening following instructions. World War II officially began for the United States on December 8, 1941 when we declared war on Japan. On December 11, 1941, Germany declared war on the U.S.

The next morning Jack went over to register for the Neighborhood Watch and I went to the Red Cross to offer my services as a volunteer. Corporations during wartime were asked to allow their employees time off to work as a volunteer for the war effort. They apparently were in great need of drivers, so I was assigned to drive a small bus and my principal assignment was to drive servicemen to their point of embarkation in New Jersey. I would pick the boys up at a locale in lower Manhattan and on the way to New Jersey, would try desperately to keep the conversation on a jovial level.

It was obvious that these young men, who had never before been off the family farm or away from their small-town homes, were now terrorized at the thought of what they would be forced into once they arrived at their base in Europe.

I brought a notepad with me and always asked if they would sign their names so I could keep in contact with them. Saying goodbye to these young men was heart wrenching, especially when we got to the pier. Here, bedlam prevailed! The Red Cross workers were serving doughnuts and coffee and there were hundreds of family members; mothers, fathers, wives holding babies, young children – all trying to be brave as they were saying goodbye to their loved ones, possibly for the last time.

After all had embarked, people were waving through their tears as the ship pulled out into the middle of the Hudson River and sailed out towards the Statue of Liberty. Some family members would stand their stoically watching until the ship was completely out of sight. Others left the pier immediately, sobbing. The Red Cross personnel would gather up their paraphernalia and all left the pier in a state of utter sadness.

This began to take its toll on me and I realized that only a close communication with God was going to carry me through. I recall stopping at a small neighborhood Catholic Church, where I went inside and prayed for well over an hour that God would give me the courage to be able to continue in this work at the Red Cross. I left that church with renewed hope and I found the closer I stayed to my Creator, the more I was able to handle the tragedies we were witnessing on a daily basis.

New Yorkers were completely transformed. As I walked to work, I would pass several newsstands where people were lined up anxiously purchasing the morning newspapers. We had no television at the time and most of our news came through the dailies. Sometimes people reading the casualty lists would begin to cry out and the sophisticated New Yorkers, who never in the past spoke to strangers, would gather round and try to offer solace to this victim of the war. We were all victims because we were all touched one way or another.

In the evenings, I worked as a volunteer at the famous Stage Door Canteen, which had been established by Broadway's most famous stars. Here, young men would come in and spend a few hours trying to forget what lay ahead as they were served sandwiches and soft drinks.

After the theaters closed at 10 o'clock, and the superstars began to arrive, it was indeed a very exciting time at the Canteen. Tallulah Bankhead was a great favorite, with her husky voice and irreverence. Claudette Colbert, Rex Harrison, Helen Hayes, Bette Davis, Jimmy Cagney, Alfred Lunt, and Lynne Fontaine all expended a great deal of time and effort at the Canteen. It was not unusual to see some of Broadway's brightest lights wearing aprons, making sandwiches or pouring coffee. My assignment was to act as hostess, greeting young men as they came in the door and making them feel welcomed. Some men wished to socialize, others wanted to sit in a quiet corner by themselves, and it often took the gentle persuasion of a group member to get them to communicate about their fears and expectations.

My job at Grant advertising was most demanding and I later learned that even there, though I didn't know it at the time, the work I was doing involved the war effort. Many Grant Advertising executives were flying back and forth to Rio de Janeiro and Buenos Aires on a frequent basis. It was extremely difficult booking these people on the airlines because all passengers were flying on priority, and since the planes had several stopovers, my passengers could be offloaded and then I would have to find some other way of getting them to their destination. I was always surprised when this happened because I would be asked to go to Washington D.C. to the Secretary of State's office, where Mrs. Shipley, who was in charge of military transportation, would immediately see me and upgrade our priority. It was only years later that I learned that the Grant Advertising people I was booking were actually FBI agents and that the Grant corporation had made it possible for them to conceal their identity.

Although Americans who were not in the military suffered very little during the war, there was some rationing. For example, one only got enough gas for emergency situations and certain groceries were rationed from time to time. If you were fortunate enough to have any nylon hose left over from peace time days, you could take them in for mending, which was a completely new experience for us.

Finally on May 8, 1945, church bells began ringing and our city began an enormous celebration. The European Theater of War was over. One week later the war with Japan was over. As all the lights came on, New York reclaimed its title as the city that never sleeps.

One day I decided to go down to the pier when the ships were coming in with our returning veterans. I hoped to see some of the boys with whom I had kept in contact while they were overseas. Unfortunately, it was not a happy experience. I saw very few and they were not the young, healthy men, I had known in 1941. Some were in wheelchairs, others on crutches or stretchers.

One of the most memorable experiences of my life happened when Jack and I sat on the curb for many hours, across from St. Patrick's Cathedral, watching the victory parade of thousands of our returning veterans. It was amazing how quickly everything seemed to get back to normal. Rosie the Riveter went home to take care of her family and it was wonderful to see countless numbers of young men once again in our streets. But after the war which was to end all wars, we needed an atomic bomb to end this one. What happened?

LESSONS LEARNED

———

In 1941 with World War II, my life changed dramatically
as I worked with the Red Cross and at the Stage Door Canteen,
witnessing tragedy almost on a daily basis. What lesson did I learn?
In the horror of war, nobody really wins.

In the same period, though, I was fortunate to obtain a position,
which made my dream of being in the travel industry possible.
This opened a whole new world to me and created an interest
in visiting the far countries of this planet
and learning about other cultures.

———

CHAPTER 5

David Enters my Life

In 1946 my marriage was coming apart. Jack had taken to gambling heavily and spent most of his free time at the track. We were spending less and less time together. As a result, I filed for divorce. Although Jack and I stayed good friends for the rest of his life, I was glad the marriage was over.

On the other hand, my position at Grant was leading to an exciting career with new challenges on an almost daily basis. We had now moved our offices from the RCA Building to one of the top floors of the renowned Empire State Building on 42nd Street. Although all of the employees in the New York office seemed to be extremely happy campers, the company was unsuccessful in attracting new clients and was therefore losing a vast amount of money. Finally Mr. Grant announced that he was sending his Vice President for Latin America, David Echols, to the New York office to clean house.

He arrived and I definitely remember the incredible impact he had on all the women in the office. He was a 6'2" very handsome Texan, and when word got around the office that his marriage was failing, there was great excitement in the female arena. This did not include me because in the first week he was in the office, he fired approximately a hundred people and when Mr. Grant's secretary called me from Chicago to tell me I had been on the list, I was obviously not enchanted with Mr. Echols. When Mr. Grant had told him that he wanted me to continue with the company, David decided that I must be one of Mr. Grant's female conquests, which there were many. What he did not know was that when Mrs. Grant was in New York, I went with her on shopping expeditions and made all arrangements for them while they were in the city – hotel reservation, dinner reservations, tickets to the theater, etc.

So now I was in a rather enviable position. The boss couldn't fire me. This infuriated David, so we simply stopped speaking to one another. His secretary would come to me with his itineraries which included travel to Latin America, South Africa and England. The following year, David hired a new secretary, Petey, who became one of my dearest friends (and still is today). Petey and I were movie buffs and would sometimes spend a weekend seeing as many as three or four pictures together.

In 1949, Petey was about to get married. When I asked her what she'd like as a wedding present, she said she wanted Dave Echols and me to take her to lunch. I said, "No way!" And Mr. Echols reacted the same. Both he and I were extremely reluctant, but she insisted, giving us no choice.

Dave took us to the 21 Club, ordered a bottle of wine and then spent the next 30 minutes telling me he thought I was the "most arrogant little snip" he ever encountered. I responded in kind. By the end of the lunch, however, Petey saw to it that we had progressed to where at least our conversation was civil.

Shortly after Petey left the company, Dave called and said, "I want you to move to the executive floor since they can never find you when they need you." I was having such a marvelous time downstairs with my media friends that I hated to move.

Years later, David always told everyone that I had never bought lunch for myself in all the time I worked at Grant. There was a Longchamps Restaurant on the first floor of the Empire State Building and many times he would see me having lunch with some of the male contingency.

Dave by this time was separated from his wife and was living at the New York Athletic Club. He was heavily involved with several women. One day, later that year, he asked me to have lunch with him so that we could work on the itinerary for his forthcoming trip to South Africa. Over lunch, I immediately told him, "If you have any thought about adding me to your stable of women, just forget about it." He laughed loudly and said, "Don't worry. I wouldn't touch you with a 10-foot pole."

Dave went off on his trip, which was a long one, and after he got back, I found myself in trouble again. In his absence, we at Grant's had gotten back into our old habits of celebrating birthdays, engagements, marriages, bar mitzvahs, and any other possible excuse for a party during working hours. One day, a group of us were having a high old time in the art department, celebrating the latest excuse du jour. Mr. Grant, Mr. Echols, and other executives were all supposed to be in Detroit at a meeting with Chrysler. They got back earlier than expected. The door to the art department swung open, and there they stood. I was sitting on the top rung of a ladder. Others later said they could never understand how I'd managed to slide past the culprits on the lower rungs and slip through a side door before Mr. Echols began a thunderous harangue. I figured I'd be fired so I went home, packed my bags, and left for Wisconsin to visit my parents. My father had bought a small resort in the Rhinelander, Wisconsin area and I thought this would be just the opportunity to visit them.

The following Saturday I was listening to the radio in Rhinelander when I heard that a small plane had hit the top floors of the Empire State Building. In desperation, I tried to telephone some of our people to question whether any of our employees had been hurt. Fortunately, Dave and a group of account executives were not scheduled to be in the office until noon that day, so they had not yet arrived when the plane hit. One of our employees, however, who was already working in the office, was badly hurt when he got on an elevator and the elevator fell.

To my surprise, a week later I received a phone call from Dave's secretary wanting to know when I'd be back at work. I came back sheepishly and resumed my responsibilities.

In 1950, I attended the Annual Grant Christmas party. It was a gala event and I had been dancing for hours. My feet were aching and I had found a quiet corner where I could be by myself for a few minutes. Suddenly Dave came up behind me and said, "You look exhausted, as though you are bored to death. Would you like to go out and have dinner?" I readily agreed. Something magical happened that night and I decided, unbeknownst to him, that someday we'd be married. Shortly thereafter, we were dating. With such a stormy beginning, it was strange to be falling in love. Our engagement stunned everyone at Grant Advertising! We were married August 1951, and spent 44 glorious years of wine and roses together, until Dave's death in 1995.

Our wedding day, August 31, 1951.

LESSONS LEARNED

———

I learned what true love is. I do know that by my association with this great man, I grew mentally, physically and spiritually over the 44 years I was privileged to share with him.

Another very important lesson was learning to adjust calmly in a crisis. This made it possible for me to overcome some serious problems that I experienced later in life.

———

CHAPTER 6

Life in Venezuela

In the first years of our marriage, we unfortunately encountered some serious problems we had not foreseen. David had two wonderful children, Susan and Bill, from his first marriage. However, Emmarie, Dave's first wife, was very bitter and she alienated us from the children until they reached maturity.

At that time, they came to us, and today they are both married, with children and they all have added a great dimension to our lives. Susan is one of my dearest friends and her children, Dana and Bret, with their families, bring great joy into my life.

After we married, Dave decided that since he didn't want to spend most of his time traveling internationally, he would leave Grant Advertising. I also moved on, joining Fugazy Travel Service as an outside representative. In this capacity, I was able to have flexible hours and travel with Dave when he went overseas on business. Then, too, I was eligible for reduced travel benefits, which was a great advantage since we spent many weekends in both Bermuda and Jamaica. Traveling was a great learning experience, which enabled me to open my own travel agency later on.

We had found an absolutely marvelous penthouse overlooking the East River and the United Nations. Although the apartment was relatively small, it had a huge terrace. We had recently acquired

Our beautiful daughter, Susan, with her husband, John O'Donnell.

two dogs. One, Sadie, a beautiful Cocker Spaniel and Susie, a funny, mischievous beagle, and because of this huge terrace, we no longer had to take them for walks and they were having an absolutely delightful time. David had not been very satisfied with the new agency he had joined, but I was not quite prepared for what was to follow.

On an early day in May, I had moved our furniture out on the terrace and had prepared a pitcher of martinis while waiting for Dave. As we sat down, enthralled by our magnificent surroundings, watching boats on the East River, he suddenly turned to me and said, "How would you like to live in Venezuela?" I replied, "That would be about as attractive to me as moving to the Arctic Circle." I thought he was kidding, but he wasn't. Due to his expertise in Latin America, he had been offered what looked like a fine opportunity to establish Pepsi Cola in Venezuela.

He waxed such great enthusiasm that I agreed to go. Since they wanted us to move soon, I took on the task of turning my travel business over to a friend. In addition, I had to make all the arrangements for our move because Dave had developed pneumonia. It was not an easy task dealing with the Venezuelan bureaucrats, obtaining the necessary visas and getting permission to bring our dogs into the country. I had managed to obtain a passage for us on the W.R. Grace Line so we could at least relax for seven days en route to our new home.

However, when we got to our cabin on the morning we were to sail, many of our friends were waiting to say good-bye and I was not a happy camper. I felt a premonition that this was not our wisest decision. As we sailed by the Statue of Liberty, I was crying hysterically. One would have thought I was never coming home again.

The second day out to sea, we were having lunch in the dining room when suddenly a crew officer beckoned to the captain who was having lunch. About 15 minutes later, the ship began to roll, dishes crashing all over the dining room. We were advised to return to our cabins until further notice. Some of the crewmembers helped us, as it was practically impossible to walk without support. We were told that we were going to the rescue of a freighter. Our ship, which had been heading into the storm with little problem, now had to turn and sail sideways. It didn't take long before I was desperately ill and for the next eight hours I was not really sure whether or not I would opt for the ship to sink. David, who was never subject to seasickness, went up to the captain's bridge with the crew and thoroughly enjoyed the spectacle of the storm from this vantage point. He brought me mashed potatoes and jiggers of vodka, which the doctor recommended I take along with the medications he was prescribing. From my bunk, I noticed Sadie and Susie were sprawled out on all fours and I decided to join them. The solidarity of the floor did give me some relief. We had finally arrived in the area where the freighter had gone down and joined several others ships in searching for survivors. All ships got into a circle and then one by one crisscrossed over to the other side. Some of the other ships had picked up survivors and we were finally notified to leave the area, as there seemed to be nothing more we could do. Once we turned and resumed our course, I began to feel better and within one day we were sailing on a calm sea.

When we reached our destination of LaGuaira, our dogs were reluctant to disembark – rightly as it turned out. The port itself was an armed camp, with soldiers toting machine guns everywhere. I tried to get David to get back on board and sail straight to New York, but without success. It took a miserable, unpleasant three hours and some healthy bribes to get past the threatening customs officers. Even then, they stole most of our collection of big band Broadway show recordings, claiming they were "subversive."

A friend, who was later to be a business associate of David's, picked us up at the port and drove us to Caracas. The road was narrow and went through the mountains. Crosses had been put up along the route in memory of those who had missed one of the many hazardous curves. (During our stay in Venezuela, a four-lane highway replaced this road.)

Caracas itself is the city of eternal spring. Orchids bloom year round, through the warm days and cool nights. Our friends had rented us a small cottage on the grounds of the Caracas Country Club, where we stayed while we looked for more permanent housing. David would leave very early in the morning. Since offices were closed from noon to 2:00 P.M. for the siesta, people worked until 7:00 P.M. David usually got home well past 8:00 P.M. The one friend I had in Caracas was extremely busy and could spend little time with me, and few people used the country club during the week. Sadie, Susie and I were left to our own resources. I can honestly say that I have never been more lonely and miserable in my entire life. Finally, I found a lovely furnished house, available for a short-term lease while its owners were in Europe. After we moved in, life improved. David was making a great many business acquaintances, and we began to entertain at home.

But life under the ruthless dictator, Perez Jimenez, was extremely depressing. We had been in our new house only a few days when the doorbell at the patio entrance rang. I was home alone. When I opened the door, a man started talking to me in Spanish. I couldn't understand him. When I failed to respond, he reached into his bag and pulled out a pair of scissors, and tried to cut the telephone wires. Frantically, I shoved him out the door and locked it behind him. Within minutes, squad cars arrived at the house and police demanded I open the door. Thank God, my neighbor saw what was going on and came to my rescue. My caller had been a representative of the telephone company, trying to collect one month's security from us as new tenants.

Shortly after my run-in with the phone company, we were having a dinner party for some of David's colleagues. One of them had left his car parked, perfectly legally in front of our house. Another vehicle came around the corner and struck his car. When the police arrived, they arrested our guest, who hadn't even been in the car when it was hit and could in no way be responsible for the accident. It took intervention from the American Embassy to find our friend and get him out of jail. Most Venezuelans didn't drive because whenever there was an accident, the driver would end up in jail. I was extremely nervous when David insisted on driving.

One of my principle problems was finding some way to pass the time. There were a good many American families in our neighborhood, and the wives spent much of their time at coffee klatches or afternoon bridge sessions. Neither activity held much appeal for me.

After exploring my options, I decided that what Caracas lacked was an exclusive men's shop. I would lease a small space and bring from New York some of the better lines of men's accessories. What I didn't know was that wealthy Venezuelan men traveled extensively and did their shopping in Paris, London and New York. So we took my losses and closed shop after a short period.

The poverty in Venezuela was ubiquitous and depressing. A few very rich families owned the country. There was no middle class. Most of the populations lived in abject poverty, living in caves and making a living any way they could. The problem was compounded by government policy that encouraged the immigration of Italians, to a point of complete over-saturation. Many of these immigrants couldn't find work and roamed the neighborhoods, often with young children in tow, trying to find carpentry or gardening work. Some had beautiful linens with them, treasures that they brought from home and now offered in exchange for a meal. I am ashamed to say many of our neighbors took terrible advantage of these desperate people. We hired a number of them to work in our garden and do odd jobs around the house. David also employed several in his office. One day, on coming home, we were horrified to find that a young man had hanged himself in the neighbor's yard. We had never seen such terrible poverty.

The opening of the Tomanaco Hotel, owned by Pan American World Airways, was the social event of the year. The famous chanteuse, Patachoy, had been engaged for the opening night gala. Her husband and manager, Arthur Lesser, was a man with a fiery disposition. He couldn't communicate in Spanish and was having a terrible time making his wishes known at the hotel. Someone suggested that he get in touch with David for help. That evening, when David and Arthur walked into the pavilion, they were surprised to see television cameras in strategic locations around the stage. Under Pat's contract, television coverage was not permitted. David finally managed to communicate with the station managers, who agreed not to televise the evening's performance.

The next crisis came when Pat walked out on stage and discovered that, because President Jimenez was in the audience, there were hundreds of armed guards around the perimeter of the pavilion with their weapons ready. Pat left the stage and found Arthur, watching from the wings. "Arthur, I cannot possibly sing. I am frightened

David, Wilbur Morrison, me and Patachou, world famous French singer,
at the opening of the Tomanaco Hotel, Venezuela, 1959.

to death of those armed guards pointing their guns directly at the
stage." Escorting her back onstage, Arthur, in his usual sardonic
style reassured her, "Don't worry. As long as you don't hit a wrong
note, they won't shoot."

After the performance, Pat and Arthur came back to our house
with some friends. Pat made one of her famous omelets. Just as we
were sitting down, the phone rang. It was Pedro Astrada, head of
Venezuelan's secret police – an elegant, handsome, soft-spoken man
with a notorious reputation for cruelty to prisoners. He wanted to
speak to Arthur. When Arthur returned to the table, he told us that
he and Pat were invited to Astrada's house. Astrada was having a
party and they wanted to meet Pat. Arthur had refused the invitation. We wondered, not surprisingly, whether he might be arrested.
It was obvious that Pat and Arthur were being followed. How, otherwise, would Astrada have known they were at our house? Thank
God, we heard nothing further about the incident.

The next night's show was to be in the hotel's ballroom. Arthur,
who was becoming more and more disillusioned with Venezuela,
came into the ballroom and once again found television cameras.
In a fury, he pulled the switch, throwing the entire ballroom into
darkness. David and I sat laughing hysterically, wondering what the
fallout would be from this latest episode. The engineers arrived and,

after a long delay that greatly annoyed the audience, they got the show going once again. Needless to say, we were somewhat relieved to say goodbye to our friends the next morning.

Xavier Cugat and his band were the next entertainers to arrive at the Tomanaco and their opening night was equally eventful. The President once again appeared. He sent an aide to request one of his favorite songs. Cugat explained that his orchestra couldn't perform this number, since they didn't know the music. Two policemen then escorted Cugat off the stage. We heard later he had been taken to the police station. Unsurprisingly, the band was delighted to get out of the country.

Life in Venezuela in the 1950s could be hazardous for your health. For example, before the country's Independence Day, the newspapers carried notices warning everyone to be under cover by 7:00 P.M. because the air force was planning a fly-by over the city and the planes would be shooting live ammunition. Luckily, we saw the notices and barricaded ourselves inside the house – a wise move since the next morning the yard was full of empty shells and shrapnel.

Our house was on a very busy intersection. Every day, there were at least two or three accidents. Finally, David went down to the police station to ask if a traffic light could be installed. A few days later, as he was leaving the house, he noticed a young boy perched on a stool at the corner of the street. David walked over and asked him what he was doing there. "Oh, Senor, this is my new job. I am the witness."

One day, a stray dog came to our door. He was starving and bedraggled, but his tail wagged engagingly. Although we worried he might pass God-knows-what to Sadie and Susie, he was such a charmer that we took him in. We named him Sam. Sam was a complete joy, and once we got him cleaned up and fed, he was quite presentable. We kept him in the patio area of the house away from the other two dogs. But one night, as we were leaving for the evening, we found that Sam had gotten upstairs and was having a romantic interlude with Sadie. Despite our best efforts, we couldn't separate the two dogs. In desperation, David suggested I call the U.S. Embassy for advice. When I explained the problem to one of the attaches, I got this haughty response, "Madam, put pepper on the male dog's nose." We did, and the problem was solved. David, who had had years of

Suzy, "Sam the Man" and Sadie in Caracas, Venezuela.

experience dealing with diplomats, always said it was the best advice he'd ever received from an American embassy.

Now that the Tomanaco Hotel was open, it became the Americans' favorite hangout. The place was always crowded, especially on the days when cruise ships were in at LaGuaira. We would gather at the outside bar by the swimming pool and watch in amusement as a steady stream of American tourists, many of them anything but elegantly dressed, dashed through the shops, looking for bargains – foolishness in this high cost country!

Robberies in the area where we Americans lived were a major problem. Presumably Venezuelans took better precautions. Shooting in self-defense could lead to a lengthy jail sentence, if the perpetrator survived long enough to make it off your property. Our first encounter with burglars began when I awoke one night to see someone coming in our bedroom. I called out to David, and the intruder ran downstairs and fled the house. We found our dogs peacefully sleeping off a dose of chemical spray. Probably we were going to be next. Once we were unconscious, the intruder could have rifled the house for several hours. And what a bonanza he would have had! As usual, clients had paid David in cash and there was about $10,000 lying on the dresser.

The next robbery happened when we were out. The robber, so disgusted by our lack of valuables, avenged himself by throwing all

our clothes on the floor and defecating on them – a common practice at the time. We made a quick trip back to New York to replenish
our wardrobes.

We started to feel slightly apprehensive every time we came
home from a night out. One evening, I walked onto our upstairs terrace to fix us both a nightcap. Suddenly, I let out a blood-curdling
scream as I saw a hand coming over the terrace railing. Dave ran out
and pulled the man onto the terrace, detaining him while I called
the police. The man was begging David to release him, saying he
couldn't understand why we were picking on him when there were
so many professionals working our block.

Finally, our kind ambassador helped us to get a guard assigned
to our house. On his first night on duty, we went to dinner with
one of the neighbors, the Embassy Military Attaché. We came home
to find that our next-door neighbor's house had been cleaned out.
Apparently a truck had pulled up in their driveway and thieves had
loaded up most of their ground floor furniture and all the silver.
When David asked our guard how this could possibly have happened while he was sitting there, the guard answered he was not
paid to guard their house.

Finally, in desperation, we gave up. We were only going to be in
Venezuela for another few months anyway. So we moved to the security of the Tomanaco Hotel. As we were preparing to leave the house,
our friends insisted that we have a garage sale to rid ourselves of the
things we wouldn't be taking back to the U.S. Of course, they used
the opportunity to do a little attic-cleaning themselves. On the day
of the sale, our garage and lawn were packed with bargains.

About 10:00 A.M. that morning, the wife of the press attaché at the
Embassy and I were relaxing on our terrace. Suddenly an Embassy
car came around the corner and Joe, her husband, was calling out to
his wife, "Ann, Ann, where is my black suit? I'm due in LaGuaira in
one hour to meet a delegate and I simply cannot find my black suit."
He had tried calling us, but our phone was inundated with calls
about the sale.

Ann, who was a very tranquil character, said blithely, "Well, I'll go
down and look. Perhaps I got it mixed up in the clothes I brought
out for the sale." Sure enough, it was the only sale we had made all
morning. We had sold Joe's good black suit for $10!

Shortly thereafter our very mean macaw apparently decided there was too much confusion in the house for his taste, so he climbed off his perch and jumped into the street. He was now about half-a-block away from the house enjoying his freedom and had no intention of being recaptured. We finally had to get a huge cage from the Animal Welfare Organization and it took the assistance of several police officers to finally bring him home.

During this time with the doors constantly being opened, our dogs, Sadie and Susie decided they would join in the merriment. When I realized they had escaped, I was frantic because the procedure for eliminating rabies in Venezuela was to come through the neighborhoods and throw poisoned meats on our lawns.

Ann called over to the Embassy and now there were three Embassy cars circling the blocks, calling out to Sadie and Susie. Finally, we located them and, thank God, they must have not been too hungry. They were well and hearty.

That night we were very glad the garage sale was finally over. After we totaled up the cost of drinks and food for the day, this garage sale proved to be one of my least successful business ventures.

Six months later, after a series of farewell parties, we flew back to New York. I still remember how absolutely delighted we were as the plane circled and started to head north.

We had to leave poor Sam behind. Sadie and Susie were coming back with us, but we couldn't bring our adopted mutt. Fortunately, our next-door neighbors, with whom Sam was very happy, adopted him. We were crushed when 10 days later, we got a letter saying Sam had run away. We had little hope for Sam's survival.

Three months later, David had to go back to Venezuela for a Pepsi Cola meeting. As he pulled up to the building, he heard what sounded almost like a human scream. Sam leapt through the open car window and landed on David's lap, wild with joy. Apparently, Sam had tracked David's car to the Pepsi Cola headquarters the day before our departure. David said later that one of the most touching experiences in his life was holding this dirty, emaciated animal, which was showering him with dog kisses. He could only imagine how much Sam had suffered over those months, without ever giving up hope that we would return. His survival was a miracle.

Luckily, the woman who operated the Christian Dior shop in the Tomanaco Hotel had known Sam from visiting our home in

Venezuela and had found him charming. She agreed to adopt him. When David last saw Sam, he was on his penthouse terrace, splendidly turned out in a jeweled collar and a very fancy leash.

LESSON LEARNED

—

*Our move to Venezuela was my first opportunity
to get to know another culture. I also learned how very privileged
we are to be Americans. We take for granted so many privileges
that no other country enjoys. Learning a new language
and associating with people who were quite different from
my America friends was enriching and rewarding,
but I recognized early on that I would not be a candidate
for a lifetime of work overseas.*

—

CHAPTER 7

I Become an Entrepreneur and Joan Crawford Contributes Greatly to my Success

In 1954, after returning to New York from Venezuela, David and I decided that this might be the right time for me to open my own travel agency.

Unfortunately, we made a poor choice when we purchased an existing agency, which had a client list that had been grossly exaggerated and was by no means the lucrative business we had expected. We had agreed that my agency, International Travel Service, would specialize in commercial accounts – a difficult route for a woman entrepreneur, I can tell you! At first, it was a scramble to find business. One of my first accounts was the Relin Public Relations Firm. They did a minimal amount of international travel, and we could only charge a five percent commission on domestic flights, so the account generated very little in the way of revenue. Nonetheless, I had put in long hours to get a space for Mr. Relin on TWA's coast-to-coast flight, which offered berths. It was the only airline with berths, making competition for these coveted spots fierce. You might ask why I bothered. My rationale was that Relin represented Pepsi Cola. If I gave the smaller firm first-rate service, they might open some important doors for me.

And that indeed was exactly what happened. One happy day, I received a phone call from Mr. Relin saying that Alfred Steele, chairman of the Pepsi Cola Company, was marrying Joan Crawford, the famous movie star. They wanted to honeymoon on the new liner, *SS United States*, which was sailing to Southampton in about three weeks. Despite their best efforts, the travel department of Pepsi, Columbia Pictures and NBC had been unsuccessful in their efforts to obtain the accommodation Mr. Steele had requested. Adrenaline pumping, I grabbed a cab and took off for the U.S. lines office in lower Manhattan. I found, to my discouragement, that not only was the entire ship booked on full deposit, but also there was a waiting list on which Al Steele's name was about 25th. I gently persuaded the steamship company's public relations department to jump Steele's name to first place on the waiting list, since the PR generated by having Joan Crawford on board would be most advantageous to the company.

Next, I decided to spend each morning at the United States line. In those days all bookings were handled by mail, so I wanted to be there when the mail was being opened in case one of the suites I needed was cancelled. I knew that it was necessary for me to be there or else the line would release the suite directly to the Pepsi Cola Company. Things were looking extremely bleak until one day, about 12 days before the sailing, a suite was cancelled and although it was not one Mr. Steele would be interested in, I asked for a 12 hour option on it. No one could understand why I wanted this, but what they didn't know was that while I was helping them with the mail, I had access to the booking charts and had made a note of the suites I needed and the names, addresses and telephone numbers of clients who were holding them. I immediately went back to my office and placed a call to Wyoming, forgetting it was three hours earlier in Wyoming. However, this very nice western gentleman answered the phone and I identified myself by giving him my name and telling him, laughingly, that "he was standing in the way of my whole career." He confirmed that he was holding suite number U80 and I told him that I had reserved a suite that was not nearly as deluxe as U80, but if he would make a switch with me, I would gladly pay for his passage. He very kindly said that he did not really care where he was, as long as the accommodation was comfortable and if I guaranteed him he would meet Joan Crawford, I could have the suite. I assured him that this could be done.

I now called the line and told them to call the gentleman from Wyoming and get a confirmation of what he told me, before he had time to completely wake up. They called me back and congratulated me for having accomplished the swap. I phoned Mr. Steele's office and when his secretary put me through to him, I advised him that I had his accommodation and since he had never heard of me, he said, "Well, I don't believe it." My response was, "Mr. Steele, please believe me because I am on my way over to get a deposit from you." When I arrived at his office, he told his secretary to call the United States line and get confirmation from them that indeed International Travel was holding this reservation for him. Mr. Steele put down the phone and in an amused voice, which I later learned to love, he said, "Alright missy, tell me the truth, how did you steal this reservation away from my travel department and all the other companies that were working on this project?" I told him what I had done, he laughed, called his secretary in, and dictated a note to his travel department saying that from now on, all Pepsi Cola business worldwide would be booked through International Travel. Needless to say, although I was a very happy camper, the travel department was not, so it was very rough going in the beginning. Eventually we became very good friends and worked well together.

It was with great trepidation that I went down to the ship the morning the Steeles were sailing. I went to the cabin to make sure all of Joan's orders had been followed and was pleased to find that all was well. The Smirnoff vodka, Bloody Mary mix, dozens of Pepsi Colas were all neatly arranged in the bar area, the flowers I had ordered were placed in strategic locations throughout the suite and most important, there was an ironing board in the bedroom, which Joan had requested. The spreads had been removed from the beds, replaced by clean, white starched sheets. Joan, who was almost neurotic about cleanliness, refused to allow spreads on the bed, since they might not have been cleaned since the last occupant had slept there. On the cocktail table in the living room was a huge container of caviar, a gift from the 21 Club. This was a great relief because I had heard how very difficult Joan was to deal with, and I was fearful she might try to get Al to transfer the Pepsi account to the agency she had been using. I now walked up to the front of the pier to await the arrival of their limousine and was very pleased at the gracious way she greeted me when Al introduced us. Joan looked spectacularly beautiful. She was wearing a simple black dress, with a beautiful broach. A pill box hat, as they were called in those days, over her hair, which was tightly pulled back. I couldn't wait to look down to see if she was wearing her famous ankle strap shoes. Yes, of course she was. She was very gracious and talkative as we walked down the pier and boarded the ship. A good number of their friends were already at the suite when we arrived. She greeted them warmly and then began a thorough inspection of the suite. I noticed her doing the finger dust test and was greatly relieved when she came to me and said that everything was perfect. She kissed me on the cheek and thanked me profusely. I said good bye to them, left the suite and ran down the pier.

Thanks to an invitation from the owner, I was allowed to board one of the tugs which would be towing the ship out into the middle of the Hudson River to turn her around and start her on her transatlantic voyage. It was wonderful to be part of the excitement from this vantage point. Bells were ringing, signaling the visitors to disembark the ship and great crowds gathered on the pier to wave and call out to the people who were now on deck, saying goodbye to their friends. Sirens sounded and massive amounts of confetti were tossed from the ship, down onto the pier. As we pulled out into the Hudson, hundreds of small boats contributed to this wild celebration. We joined this merry group and accompanied the ship out as far as the Statue of Liberty. Through the owner's binoculars I could see Joan and Al, still standing on the deck and waving. It was a bright, beautiful day and one of the most memorable experiences of my life. I was ecstatic that everything had gone so well.

When the Steeles arrived from Europe I was anxious to know whether all the hotel reservations and plans I had made for them had met their expectations. Joan called to say that the entire trip was flawless. However, once again I was nervous when she asked me to come to the apartment to join her for breakfast the following day. She asked me to bring with me the itinerary of their forthcoming trip to Africa. I arrived at their apartment on upper 5th Avenue and she greeted me at the door. She was wearing a simple flowered cotton dress, with a beautiful apron. She asked that I remove my shoes before entering the apartment and handed me a pair of slippers. All of the carpets in the entire apartment were white. She then gave me a guided tour of the first floor and I was amazed to see that all this beautiful furniture in the living room was covered with plastic. I assumed this was due to the fact that they had just recently moved into the apartment, but was amazed months later when had not been removed.

Joan escorted me into the beautiful kitchen where she had set a table for two. We conversed while she was making an omelet. As she began to beat the eggs with her wire spatula, I saw for the first time what an extremely tense person she was. She served a lovely breakfast and then we began to go over the itinerary. Several times she asked me if I would make a change to something she did not agree with. I explained to her that I could not do this because the itinerary had already been approved by Al and the other members of Pepsi who were going on the trip and was already in the works. I said if she wanted to make changes, Al would have to approve it. Reluctantly she picked up the phone and called Al. Her voice at the beginning of the conversation was very loving, but when he refused her request, her voice became more and more harsh. Finally, irately, she slammed the phone down. I do not react well to tension, so I found that when I left her, I would have to take a very long walk to recover my equilibrium. We had many such meetings, since on every trip she wanted to go over all details with me personally. Nevertheless, although it was very difficult for me to be in Joan's presence, she turned out to be the truest of friends. It seemed as if she recommended my agency to everyone she met and was responsible for us obtaining the NBC and RCA accounts. It was also through her efforts that I handled some of the arrangements for the entourage that would be attending the Grace Kelly wedding in Monaco.

The Steele travel arrangements were often most unusual. On one occasion, Al called from Rome to say he would appreciate it if, on their flight to Nairobi the next day, I could arrange to have the all seats in the plane's first class section removed and two beds installed. They also wanted to have the section curtained off, to ensure complete privacy. Al explained that he was exhausted and had to make an important speech on their arrival. After a little thought I decided that I'd better go straight to the top with this one, so I called the chairman of British Overseas Airlines. I explained I was calling on behalf of the chairman of the Pepsi Cola Company, and when Sir William came on the line, I made it clear up front that cost was no object in what we were requesting. I outlined in detail what the Steeles wanted and at the end of my monologue, there was what seemed like an interminable transatlantic silence. At last, Sir

Joan Crawford, Al Steele and me after Joan declared that the suite for their honeymoon trip to Europe was "perfect!"

William spoke and with true British humor inquired, "Mrs. Echols, do you happen to have any preferences for the color of the curtain?" The plane arrived in Rome, altered to meet our specifications, and the Steeles were able to rest comfortably on their way to Nairobi. I've often wondered what Pepsi stockholders would have said if they had seen the size of the five-figure check we wrote to the airline.

All of that, however, was a walk in the park.

Where does an 800-pound gorilla sit? Anywhere she wants. This was Joan Crawford's philosophy of life. One night, my husband and I went out to dinner with the Steeles, and Joan insisted on ordering the meal for her guests. She decided we were all to have the duck with chocolate sauce. David and Al refused at first, but thanks to her persuasive powers, they decided to comply. I refused outright, which did not ingratiate me to her, but the next day I was the only one able to be up and about.

Joan's eyes said it all. Anyone who has seen one of her films can understand that. When she was angry, she had a glare that could terrify a tiger, but a moment later, those same eyes could knock you over with her charm. Her hatreds were legendary. One night we attended a screening of "What Ever Happened to Baby Jane?" in which Joan starred with Bette Davis, whom she especially detested. Joan was extremely uptight at the screening and tried to calm herself by knitting. The clicking of the needles went faster and faster as the movie progressed, much to the disturbance of everyone around her. At one point, I whispered to David that the makeup department had done a wonderful job making Bette Davis (who was three years older than Joan) look like an old hag. Joan, never missing a stitch, said, "Oh no dear, that's all Bette." Given her temper I was doubly glad she never had a single harsh or mean word to say to me.

Joan was such a perfectionist that it could take her two or three hours to get ready to cross the street to visit a neighbor. At the time when I was working with her, she was in her fifties, but had kept her youthful figure. This was due in part to a daily massage she underwent that was so rigorous, few people other than professional athletes could have withstood it. She could put away tremendous amounts of vodka without gaining any weight. There was always an extra pair of hose in her handbag because heaven forbid anyone should catch her with a run in her stocking. In contrast, Al was a laid back, completely relaxed man who, until he married Joan, enjoyed life to the fullest. He loved people and was very popular with all the employees of Pepsi. This was a complete contrast to Joan's hyper-personality.

When Joan traveled, depending on the length of the trip, her luggage could consist of anywhere between 10 and 25 large suitcases, hatboxes, a cosmetic case and a large jewelry case, which she had to hand carry. Needless to say, I had to be extremely careful not to make any mistakes when handling the Steele's luggage. Airline special services would have to be notified of their arrival at the airport so that someone would put them in the VIP room immediately and make sure they were pre-boarded. If Joan's two French poodles were coming along, a special seat had to be reserved for them. Arrangements also had to be made for airline personnel to meet them at their destination and escort them directly to their limo. God help everyone involved, especially me, if Joan entered her hotel suite and did not find a supply of Smirnoff Vodka and Pepsi, vases of fresh flowers throughout the entire suite and an ironing board set up in her bedroom. Despite her aristocratic bearing and demands, she never totally abandoned her difficult, impoverished roots. One day, I arrived at the Ambassador East Hotel in Chicago shortly after the Steele's arrival and found Joan, still in her travel clothes, on her hands and knees, scrubbing the bathroom floor.

Although Joan was very receptive to whatever plans I made for their trips, I saw two sides of her. We were very close friends but I must say, on only one occasion, did I see her when she was ecstatically happy. We were up in her bedroom and she was packing for her next trip. The phone rang. Immediately her voice changed and became very soft. She motioned to me to leave the room. I went downstairs and approximately half an hour later, she came dancing down the stairs, laughing a deep laugh I had never heard before. She was waving her arms and saying, "There is a man, oh yes, there is a man, Clark Gable is a man," as she continued dancing around the first floor. Apparently, Joan was madly in love with Clark Gable for many years and was saddened by the fact that he wisely refused to marry her. Although they went their separate ways, they still had a warm relationship right up to the time of Clark Gable's death.

The dark side of Joan pertains to her adopted children. The twins, Cathy and Cynthia, did not live with Joan and Al; they resided in an apartment across the street with their nanny. They visited Joan only when she so requested. It was obvious that they, too, could not relax around their mother. One never knew when her explosive temper might give way and so they were very quiet when in the presence of "mommy dearest." Christopher was a very shy, lovely boy, and I especially felt sorry for him. I saw very little of him because he eventually ran away from home and had gone to live with Joan's former chauffeur and his wife, who loved him very much. Al was in favor of allowing him to stay with these people, but Joan vehemently disagreed. Unfortunately, he was then sent to a detention center for young delinquents. Christina was a beautiful girl whom I met only on one or two occasions. She had come to the apartment, apparently in desperate need of money, and Joan refused her. However, as she was leaving, after Joan had gone upstairs, I saw Al put something in her hand, which I presumed was money. Growing up with Joan must have been extremely difficult. She was as relentlessly demanding of them as she was of herself.

In September 1959, Joan called and asked if we would stop by for cocktails before we left for New Jersey, where we spent our weekends in the summertime. I complied reluctantly and arrived at the apartment a few minutes earlier than scheduled. Joan was upstairs and I was reading a magazine when Al came into the apartment. I was shocked at his appearance. He looked haggard and worried. Of course, as soon as he saw me he became his usual gracious, affable Al. Joan came downstairs and shortly after the maid came in with a cart of beautiful hors d'oeuvres, caviar and smoked salmon and began fixing plates for us. Al quietly requested that since he did not feel well, he would like a glass of milk and would forgo the hors d'oeuvres. Joan immediately began shoving a plate towards him, saying he must at least try a little. He however stood his ground and after about 15 minutes, Joan grudgingly called the maid to bring him a glass of milk. As we were driving out to Jersey, I began to cry and said I did not think Al would survive the tension of living with Joan.

They were leaving for Bermuda on a nine o'clock flight Sunday morning. At about 10:30 A.M. the phone rang and it was Joan. I was surprised to hear her voice because they should have been airborne at this time. Imagine the shock when she said, in a calm, unemotional voice, "Evelyn dear, Al died last night, please come in as soon as you can." I guess because I could not believe this, I asked her to repeat what she said, which she did. David and I hurriedly dressed and got to the apartment around noon. By this time the Pepsi Cola Board was there and Joan was acting as though she were having a party. When she finally went upstairs I followed her and said "Joan, you don't have to do this, people expect you to be grieving." Her response was, "I'll grieve and cry alone." Not once did I see her shed a tear, not even at the funeral. After Al's death, Joan remained on the Pepsi Board for sometime, but her travels were much curtailed.

Another dimension of my travel career began one day when my husband and I were walking down 5th Avenue and ran into a friend of David's – Tom O'Neil of the General Tires family and, at the time, owner of WOR-TV, Channel 9, in New York. Tom mentioned that WOR was considering the possibility of introducing a travel show and asked if I would like to audition for it. Since I now had reached the point where I never said no to a possible opportunity, I agreed. On the day of the audition, I was extremely frightened, since I had never even sat in front of a camera before. I was sure that I would not be chosen, especially when I noticed there were quite a number of professionals being tested.

On the set of my WOR-TV Christmas show, with Sadie and Suzy helping me to convince our audience that "It's Fun to Travel!"

However, the following day I received a telephone call saying I had indeed been selected and I would begin doing the show the following month. It was a talk show format where I would interview traveling VIPs, including celebrities such as Eleanor Roosevelt, movie stars, United Nations delegates, and many United State Senators. Since in those days, all shows were live, when you boo booed, you did it in sight of your entire audience. And boo booed I did. I had begun hosting one show a week, but since it was so easy to get travel sponsors for this show, I eventually ended up on the air five half-hours a week and again on Sunday from 9:30–10:00 P.M. This went on for two years, until September of 1960 when we left New York for Chicago.

LESSONS LEARNED

———

*When I dared, in 1954, to announce that I was going to become
a woman entrepreneur by opening a commercial travel agency
in New York, I learned many lessons. If I had realized
the incredible resistance I would encounter, I probably
would not have had the courage to try,
but I did and I succeeded.*

*Joan Crawford, all by herself, was a lesson in life.
From her I learned to extend my friendships
and be more helpful to others.*

*Also during this period we began our world travels,
not only a broad learning experience,
but also some of the happiest days of my life.*

———

CHAPTER 8

Our Happy Move to Chicago

In 1960 Bob Allen, president of the agency where David worked – Fuller, Smith and Ross – met with us and asked if we would be interested in going to Chicago for a two year period so that David could establish their new Chicago office. He was concerned that I might not want to make this drastic move.

Both he and David were surprised when I said I would be overjoyed to make such a move. I was tired. The strain of operating my travel agency and hosting the television show had become stressful. So I was delighted to sell the agency and notify the station I was leaving New York. Illinois was my home and this move would bring me closer to my family. My parents were now living at a small fishing resort that they had purchased to accommodate their friends. My brother, Coleman, was living on the family farm, where I had been born. Kenneth lived in northern Michigan. Unfortunately both Coleman and Kenneth died at early ages. Bob lives in Alaska and Gloria, my sister, in northern Wisconsin. I am very fortunate that I also have a large number of nieces and nephews who visit me frequently.

In July, 1960 I boarded the 20th Century Limited with our two dogs and was off to Chicago. David had gone out earlier. A dear friend, Budd Jacks, was the general manager of a hotel and we lived there until I found an apartment. For the next few weeks I couldn't

Off to Chicago and a farewell to Terry Higgins who had been Vice President of our travel agency.

believe it. I had so much time on my hands and I was thoroughly enjoying the luxury of doing nothing. Our apartment in the hotel had two terraces, so Sadie and Susie were also delighted with their new environment. Within a month I located a beautiful condominium at 910 North Lake Shore Drive. This fabulous glass building was designed by the world famous architect, Mies van der Rohe. We had a magnificent view of Lake Michigan from all windows. David was extremely busy preparing his office in the Wrigley Building and on September 1st, he celebrated with a gala opening.

Once again, Joan Crawford was responsible for our wonderful reception in Chicago. I had not been here more than 10 days when I received a telephone call from Mrs. Loyal Davis, mother of Nancy Reagan. She had received a phone call from her good friend Joan, asking her to see that we were properly introduced into the Chicago scene. Edie Davis became one of my closest friends. She was an amazing woman. She had been a soap opera queen before she married Loyal. Our first meeting occurred when she called to introduce herself and then told me she had had a recent fall and asked if I would accompany her to a Board Meeting of the Chicago Mental Health Society. I met her at her home and we went on down to the office. The Board of Directors of this organization was very prestigious. Edie introduced me to the entire Board and then stood up and, without asking for a vote, announced "We have a new Board member, Evelyn Echols, who has just arrived from New York." I was

The great Edie Davis, mother of Nancy Reagan, became one of my most enthusiastic supporters and a very close friend.

dumbfounded. First of all at her audacity in declaring I was a Board member without asking for a vote. And second, I had never served on a charity Board before. As the meeting progressed, I learned that the society was well over $100,000 dollars in debt and that the President, Russell Baird, a distinguished lawyer, had borrowed this money and personally signed a note for it. The note was coming due in 60 days and Russell was not exactly happy about the prospect of having to pay off this loan. That was an enormous amount of money in 1960. I came home wondering how I could be helpful and finally decided to call on Joan. I told her the story and asked if she would be willing to bring a group of Hollywood stars to Chicago for a "Joan Crawford's Star Ball for Mental Health." As usual, she immediately compiled. I notified Edie of our good fortune and of course the Board of Directors was enchanted with the idea.

We decided that if we were to net the $100,000, the price of the ticket would have to be exorbitant for that time. So it was decided that if Joan could bring 15 stars to Chicago, we could sell 15 star tables at $10,000 per table. I knew that if we were to realize this kind of revenue we would need to generate great advanced publicity.

Governor Winthrop and Jeannette Rockefeller hosted the Chicago Board of Directors of the Mental Health Association at their Winrock Estate in Little Rock, Arkansas.

I called on the President of the National Association of Mental Health, Jeanette Rockefeller, wife of Winthrop Rockefeller, who later became Governor of Arkansas. I asked if she would chair this event and then got up the courage to ask her if I could possibly bring our Board and members of the press to their magnificent Winrock estate for a weekend. Winthrop Rockefeller called me back, and although he was not delighted with the idea, he agreed. Several corporations agreed to fly the group to Little Rock where private Rockefeller planes flew us out to the estate. This proved to be one incredibly successful publicity promotion. We had full page stories in all of our newspapers for days on end, which resulted in phone calls coming in from people who wished to buy star tables.

Joan had given us a partial list of the stars who would be coming, which enhanced our position since a great number of people were willing to pay the price to be seated at their favorite star's table. The world famous Cesar Romero, Cliff Robertson and Dina Merrill, Merv Griffin, Mr. and Mrs. Robert Cummings, John Forsythe, Sebastian Cabot, Virginia Graham, Dorothy Kilgallen, Johnny Ray and Celeste Holm had agreed to come. Kookla, Fran and Ollie, Chicago's most famous television stars, along with Wally Phillips, were also in attendance and of course, Jeannette and Winthrop Rockefeller added

Joan Crawford and Peggy Goldwater,
the Senator's wife, at "Joan Crawford's
Star Ball for Mental Health."

At the Ball with Hollywood star,
Celeste Holm.

to the luster of the evening. Edie had made up her mind that this gala would emulate the glamour of the Academy Awards. Mayor Daley cooperated. The event was to take place in the magnificent Hilton Hotel ballroom. The limousines were lined up along the Michigan Avenue Bridge. They pulled up in front of the hotel, the stars stepped out onto the red carpet and Merv Griffin, who acted as the emcee for evening, introduced them to the television public. Hundreds of people were waiting in front of the hotel to greet these illustrious guests. It was a night to remember and needless to say, Russell Baird was one happy camper that evening. He became one of our very closest friends, even though I constantly reminded him that he owed $100,000.

Due to the great success of "Joan Crawford's Star Ball for Mental Health," I was elected to the National Board in Washington D.C. later that year. This resulted in my attending many Board meetings in Winrock and the Washington area. As a matter of fact, on the day President Kennedy was assassinated I was in Washington receiving an award for my work for the National Association. I was on my way to the airport when the driver notified me of the President's death. For the next eight hours, Washington National Airport – now Reagan Airport – was completely closed down. Thousands of people were walking around the airport in a complete state of shock; some sobbing, others sitting silently reading prayer books. Fortunately for me, a very dear and long time family friend, Father O'Shaughnessy, appeared. He was also on his way to Chicago and was a great solace to me during those trying hours. It was only after the President's body arrived at Andrews Air Force base that Washington National Airport was allowed to function again.

As a result of our relationship with Dr. Loyal and Edie Davis, we were invited to visit the Reagans on a trip to the West Coast. When we arrived, we were greeted by Nancy and Ronnie. Nancy took me into the library where over cocktails and hors d'oeuvres, we spent a lovely two hours getting acquainted. This gave Ronnie and David an opportunity to discuss Ronnie's forthcoming campaign for Governor of the State of California. David was quite knowledge-able about the political world, since in his youth he had worked on Lyndon Johnson's political campaign when he was running for office in Texas. Fuller, Smith and Ross had also handled Barry Goldwater's quite disastrous campaign. As we were learning, David turned to me and said, "This guy is a hell of a lot smarter than they are giving him credit for. He might even be President one day."

Joan hosted another equally successful "Stars for Mental Health Ball" for us the following year and Bob Hope was our guest at that event.

In 1970, I suggested to Jeannette Rockefeller that we might help the Mental Health Association by offering a very exclusive, high-priced European tour, with Jeannette serving as the hostess. She decided this was a fine idea. I knew that even though Jeannette would attract a large clientele, the trip had to be so outstanding that what we were offering could not be duplicated by an ordinary tour operator. Through the Rockefeller tour connections in New York, I was able to take a trip overseas to work out an itinerary which included Greece, Italy, France and England. Again, I called on my friend, Joan, and she arranged to have some members of the British theater meet with our group.

At Joan Crawford's request, J. Paul Getty hosted our Mental Health Association group at his magnificent estate in Surrey, England.

Most importantly, she convinced J. Paul Getty that he should entertain the group at his fabulous estate in Surrey. Although he was notorious for being parsimonious when he entertained, he certainly extended himself for us. Luckily, Sergeant Shriver was then our Ambassador to France so I visited with him at the Embassy and convinced him that it would be lovely if he and Maria would invite our group to their home for dinner and also include some of their French friends. This was another huge success. In Greece, the government hosted several beautiful events for us, as was true in Rome. Having been in the travel business for many years, I realized early on that there were not enough first class seats on any plane to accommodate our group. A visit with Mr. Aristotle Onassis, who owned the airline, resolved this problem. I requested that he remove the seats from the first class section and turn it into a cocktail area so that the entire party would be in tourist class, as it was known then. Jeannette, who was an incredibly gracious hostess, made this trip truly memorable.

It was now 1980 and we were all amazed when David's predication came true. Ronald Reagan was elected President of the United States. Later that year, I heard rumors that he intended to appoint a committee to advise him on women's business affairs. I casually mentioned to Edie that I would love to be on such a committee and we talked no more about it, but still I was utterly amazed when a friend of mine called me and said I was being checked out by the FBI because the President was considering me for this committee. I was delighted beyond words when I received notice that I had been selected. I arrived at the White House for a swearing in ceremony and had the opportunity to meet other members of the committee. Bay Buchanan, sister of Pat Buchanan, was Chairman of our Board and she was a sheer delight. Knowledgeable, charismatic, witty and extremely well organized. She later told me that they were beleaguered by letters from Senators and Congressman, endeavoring to get one of their constituents on our committee. So as they were trying to make a decision, they came across my application and as Bay later told me "we came upon yours and when we noticed that you were recommended by Nancy Reagan, we decided that it would not be good for our health to refuse your application." Nancy was always there for me. As a matter of fact, she even invited us to a State dinner honoring the Duke and Duchess of Luxembourg. Because of the limited number of people attending these dinners, one cannot imagine the pressure from constituents who want an invitation.

On one occasion, the President joined our committee for lunch and asked that we introduce ourselves and state who sponsored us for the committee. My response was, "It started with your mother-in-law and then Nancy." Ronny, like everyone else, immediately began to laugh and proceeded to tell very funny stories about Edie.

One early rainy morning, I was on my way to church and passed a building where someone had been dispossessed. Meager possessions were scattered on the sidewalk. The rain turned into a very heavy downpour. I entered the building and asked the telephone operator who owned this sad collection. She said it was an elderly woman but she had no idea where she had gone. I turned around, went home, and called Edie. Within an hour, she had awakened the "powers to be" in Chicago, including the Mayor and Senator Percy, who were spending the weekend in Chicago, and the publishers of the three major newspapers, the *Chicago Tribune*, the *Sun-Times*, and the *Daily News*. Much to the chagrin of the building owners, photographers had gathered and were shooting pictures of the saturated furnishings and the building with the address prominently displayed. Monday's papers all carried the story on the front page. We were able to locate the woman, who was being cared for by Catholic

To Evelyn Echols
With best wishes, Ronald Reagan

With President Reagan when I was a member of his Interagency Committee on Women's Business Enterprise.

Charities at this point. Edie followed through until the woman was comfortably ensconced in a modest apartment. Very often, Edie and Loyal would take underprivileged children to Cubs baseball games. They were involved in many charitable causes, which they rarely discussed. She had many friends, yet a good number of detractors, due in part, I believe, to the fact that Edie said whatever was on her mind and was completely unabashed about expressing an unpopular opinion.

David and I were most unhappy when Dr. Loyal retired and they moved permanently to their home in Phoenix. Loyal died shortly thereafter. The last time I saw dear Edie was when I visited her on one of my trips to the area. The nurse told me she doubted she would know me. I stood by her bed for some period of time, calling out her name and repeating mine. Suddenly she awakened, sat up and said, "It's a hell of a long time since I heard from you" and fell back into her semi-conscious state.

Nancy and I corresponded occasionally after Edie's death. Never did I feel sorrier for anyone than I did for her when Ronnie was diagnosed with Alzheimer's disease and lived with it for so many years. Theirs was such a beautiful, all consuming love affair.

LESSONS LEARNED

———

*Through the good auspices of Joan Crawford, I met Edie Davis
and became active in the mental health movement,
a new experience from which I learned that charity work
is especially rewarding. Since then I have stayed involved,
serving on numerous boards and committees.*

*During this period, I also had the great broadening experience
of serving on President Reagan's Women's Advisory Board,
which gave me great insight into how Washington
and the White House operate.*

———

CHAPTER 9

Cast Thy Bread upon the Water

For many years, I had been praying to God for a meaningful involvement where I could render service to needy individuals. Sometimes you find answers to your prayers not by searching but by tripping.

I never expected to find the calling that kept me deeply involved, quite happy, and very busy for the next 36 years. The opportunity was given to me in the strangest way.

One evening we were at a party at a friend's house. Two of the guests were family court judges. They were discussing the problem of getting juvenile delinquents who were serving time to take an interest in education. I made some comments to the effect that these kids were most likely school dropouts and vocational education might be a promising approach to get them involved. They might be attracted to the travel industry, in which I'd worked for many years. There is a dream quality to a travel career since it affords the opportunity to see the world and visit places one only dreams of visiting.

Like most party banter, I forgot about this conversation until one of the judges called and asked if I'd be willing to teach a travel course at a girl's reformatory, as these institutions were called at the time. I decided to take on the challenge. I am grateful to God that I did so. It led me in directions I never could have imagined at the time.

I was to teach at the House of Good Shepherd, a Roman Catholic institution run by nuns, to which first time offenders were sent by the family court. I started my first day of teaching with much trepidation. I had never taught before and I questioned my ability to inspire these girls. Time and effort were needed to prepare for an entry-level position in the travel industry. Could I get them fixed up enough to make it work?

A policeman met me at the gate and took me to meet Mother Helene, a remarkable, compassionate woman whom I learned to cherish. Given her schedule, I have no idea how she survived. Besides her regular daily duties, which were enough to crush a horse, she spent many a night sitting up with frightened, despondent new arrivals.

Mother Helene told me that she had chosen 15 girls for the course and took me to meet them. She introduced me and left. I noticed nervously that she locked the door behind her. Immediately, a tall young woman with a hostile attitude came up to me and said belligerently, "So, dearie, you're going to teach us the travel business? Now, you tell me, could you travel from Chicago to New York to Los Angeles and back to Chicago with only one nickel in your pocket? Could you, huh?" I said I probably couldn't do that. "Well, I did!" she sneered, and sternly advised me she might be able to teach me the travel business.

Harriet was the leader of the pack, no doubt about that. And she clearly was going to be trouble. I was more encouraged by the attitude of some of the others. I told them that a wonderful world awaited them if they'd apply themselves and learn what they could about this industry, which always needed young people and didn't require a college degree to get started. The other girls were intrigued. Harriet was not. In fact, she persistently disrupted class. I got the feeling that she'd signed up for the course merely to avoid after-school chores.

I checked on Harriet's background. She'd been arrested several times, but she was highly charismatic and always managed to convince the authorities that she was innocent. That's how she became eligible for the House of Good Shepherd – she had no record. I've often thought how lucky it was that she wasn't sent to a state reformatory. If she had been, she would have been lost. She seemed prone to trouble and thoroughly enjoyed conflict. With her nasty attitude, she undoubtedly would have spent a good deal of time being disciplined by prison guards who would not have been as understanding as Mother Helene and her staff.

The girls were a real challenge because I never knew what to expect. On my fourth visit, a policeman met me at the door and took me to the superintendent's office. The policeman asked if I was aware that I was not allowed to bring indelible ink into a penal institution. I hadn't known that, and I admitted to having several bottles of ink in my file cabinet. They told me the girls had broken into the file cabinet, stolen the ink, and used it to tattoo themselves. The authorities were not pleased with me.

When I went back to the classroom, I noticed they were all wearing shirts with sleeves and slacks. Most of them were giggling. They were waiting to see how I would handle the situation. I told them that they might not find this so funny when they went applying for work, that employers didn't look favorably on body art, and that it was extremely expensive to have it medically removed. I then refused to discuss it further. They looked like a group of whipped puppies. I could tell they had been looking forward to a more heated discussion.

There were days when I had to be especially careful about how I handled them. I usually brought them small treats and tried to encourage them with compliments or awards for special efforts. They would always ask for chocolate, which I only brought on rare occasions since I felt they were hyper enough. I substituted cookies and nuts, which were always most welcomed.

I realized quickly that I couldn't develop this program all by myself. I asked for help from friends at American Express, Cunard Steamship Line, Pan American World Airways, and TWA. They all accepted the challenge. Maxwell Coker, who was then manager of the American Express office in Chicago, was one of the first to address the class. His background was in theater, and he had spent many years in England. The girls found his British accent enthralling. He had a great sense of humor and called me after his first lecture, greatly amused, saying that this was the first time he'd given a lecture when every eye was on his trouser fly.

I got personally involved with many of my students. I found I could empathize with them, and we became good friends. At least 10 of them were really very bright. Many were at the House of Good Shepherd because they were runaways. Some had been abused as children. Incestuous rape at an early age was not uncommon. Several had turned to prostitution to support themselves. Trying to give them a solid sense of self-worth was our greatest challenge. I gathered clothes from my friends for them, and Mother Helene very sensibly allowed us to do makeup demonstrations.

The girls were also my greatest critics. I never went to the House of Good Shepherd without having my hair done or not dressing in a way that I thought they might like. Sometimes they'd approve, and sometimes I'd hear comments like, "Ye gods, where did you get that?" We tried to teach them to dress in conservative business clothes once they found jobs. But sometimes after a girl found a position, I'd get a call from her employer saying that she had arrived at work in bright red stockings or a tight miniskirt – long before the mini became trendy.

We had nearly completed our first course without any major crises when one morning, at about 2:00 A.M., our doorman woke us up with a phone call, saying that three young women were down in the lobby asking for me. I asked him to put one of them on the phone, and sure enough, it was three runaways from the House of Good Shepherd. At my request, the reluctant doorman escorted the three ragamuffins to our door and was astonished when I told them to come in. They were carrying their clothes in paper bags. They'd been sleeping in a car for several days, were filthy and hadn't eaten in 24 hours. I sent them off to the bathroom to wash up while I made a huge pan of scrambled eggs. Dave and I sat and watched as they demolished all the food in sight, including two loaves of bread.

The next step was to get them to agree to go back to the institution before the police caught up with them. I was worried that the House of Good Shepherd might refuse to take them back, and that they'd be sent to a state reformatory, where conditions were horrifying. I put the youngest one to bed on our sofa and called a friend of ours in the building. She agreed to let the other two stay in her apartment until morning. I wanted them to get some rest before we decided our next move. After lengthy negotiations, the girls finally agreed to go back to the House of Good Shepherd if we would go with them, which we did. Due to Mother Helene's kindness, the incident went unreported and didn't affect their records.

At the end of the year, the class was due to graduate. I felt I should do something really special for this occasion, since this was probably the first time any of them had actually applied themselves to education. I went to see Pat Patterson, then chairman of United Airlines.

I asked if United could possibly see their way to making a plane available to take the girls on a one or two-hour flight over Chicago and serve them lunch on board. It took a little gentle persuasion to convince Mr. Patterson that this was a good idea.

Then there was the problem of outfitting the girls for the occasion. The Marshall Field's store and hairdressers from Elizabeth Arden contributed to the clothes and services. It was a very presentable group that took off for the airport that morning. When we arrived, I was astonished to find dozens of media present. Mr. Patterson had advised his company's public relations department of the event, and the PR people had spread the word. Representatives from the Associated Press, NBC, CBS, WGN, and *Time* magazine boarded the plane with us, as did several judges from family court. To top it off, the famous singer, Patty Page, had called and asked if she could come along. The girls were ecstatic to be in her presence. They had a gloriously exciting day, giving the judges quite a hard time, of course. There was no question; the flight strengthened their determination to find careers in travel and tourism.

Even Harriet's attitude had improved little by little during the course. She seemed less tough and hostile and more cooperative. Harriet had a beautiful figure, but a huge disfigured nose marred her face. After some thought, I asked her if she'd like it if I could arrange plastic surgery for her. This tough, strong, aggressive girl, who never displayed any emotion except anger, broke down sobbing. Through her tears, she told me that from the moment she'd entered the first grade, her classmates had yanked her nose and teased her unmercifully.

Well, now I had a commitment that had to be met. I approached Dr. Ira Tresley, a noted plastic surgeon, and explained the case. I told him jokingly, "I need a free nose job. Otherwise, I'll go out and campaign for socialized medicine!" He laughed and said I probably would. He asked me to bring Harriet to his office. He examined her and told her he'd do the surgery. I took her to the hospital the night before the surgery and stayed with her until she was sedated. She was so frightened that I thought she might run away had the opportunity arose.

The operation was a complete success. A week after surgery, Dr. Tresley carefully removed her bandages, gently applied a touch of makeup to cover the bruises, and handed her a mirror. She looked at her new face, started to laugh wildly, and then broke into heart-rending tears. Dr. Tresley had to sedate her before we left.

We'd arranged for the teachers of the course, Mother Helene, and some of Harriet's friends to meet us at a nearby restaurant for Harriet's coming-out party. As we walked down the street, she kept looking at her profile in store windows, saying, "I can't believe this is me!" The group brought her appropriate gifts of nosegays and decorative handkerchiefs. From that day on, her personality changed. She became more cheerful, less argumentative, and even began to take an interest in the other girl's problems, something she had never done before.

After graduation, we faced a new challenge. Harriet was one of the first girls to be released and she could easily go either way; straight or back to her previous life. We had to find her a job in a hurry. My darling husband came to my rescue again, agreeing to employ Harriet to handle travel arrangements for corporate executives in his ad agency. No one, except for the office manager, knew anything about her background. Dave kept me informed regularly about Harriet's progress. She was doing very well – always punctual, pleasant and willing to take on any assignment. The only problem was that she seemed shy and antisocial, refusing all invitations to go to lunch with other employees. I called her and asked her to stop by our apartment, and asked her what the problem was. "Who knows how to eat in a restaurant?" she answered. This was so startling to me. Who would have thought of this? But, of course, she had never in her life sat down to a meal with linens on the table.

Dave and I decided that we should invite her to dinner at our house on several occasions, which proved helpful. But we made a mistake when we asked her to a cocktail party. She drank too much. I later invited her out to an upscale restaurant for lunch. Over time she began to feel self-assured and more comfortable. Thereafter, she began to accept invitations from co-workers to meet socially.

However, her old life kept catching up with her. Former friends would wait for her to leave the office and try to sell her drugs. The strain was starting to take its toll on her. One day, she stopped by the apartment, unannounced, pale and obviously in terrible turmoil. She pulled up a chair to the window, sat down with her back to me, and said, "Mrs. Echols, you have done for me all you're ever going to do until I tell you my background."

For the next hour, she talked about how she had lived after she left home at the age of 13. It was not a pretty story: prostitution, car thefts, pilfering anything she could in order to live. By the time she was finished, she was in tears. She got up from her chair and said, "I guess you'll never want to see me again." I put my arms around her and told her that I felt just the same about her as I always had – in fact, I appreciated her all the more, knowing what she'd been through and how far she had risen from the past. I made her lunch and sent her back to the office. From that day forward, she seemed to bloom.

I was delighted when Harriet agreed to give the keynote speech for the graduating class at the House of Good Shepherd the year after her own graduation. Dr. Tresley also took part in the ceremony, as did Eunice Shriver, President Kennedy's sister, and members of the travel industry. To Dave's amazement, he learned that Harriet had enrolled in a marketing course at Loyola University and was going to class with seasoned marketers. Dave worried the course would be too advanced for her. He offered to make other arrangements with the university. She refused his intervention and went on to graduate.

Harriet was doing so well and then disaster struck. She was out on her first date with a young man, a newspaper representative who called on Dave's agency. As they were walking down Rush Street on a Sunday afternoon, they passed a group of prostitutes on a street corner. The girls recognized Harriet and ran over to greet her. Her date walked away. Again, Dave saved the situation by arranging to transfer Harriet to the agency's New York office. When she arrived in New York, she called me and said, "Mrs. Echols, that's the first time I've ever walked though an airport when the police didn't have me in handcuffs."

Harriet did well in New York and eventually married into a large, delightful family that loved and cherished her for the first time in her life. We kept close touch for several years. But then I began to see that I was, for her, a reminder of the old dark years. I told her that I thought it would be best for us to break off our relationship, but that I would always be there for her if she needed me. She agreed, and we parted friends. I have not heard from her since.

Shortly after my first group was released from the House of Good Shepherd, Dave got a call asking him to make sure that I stayed home on the morning of Mother's Day. Since I usually went to church that day, I couldn't understand why Dave kept insisting that I attend a later service – until the doorbell rang. Standing there were six of my former students. They gave me the most beautiful jade necklace from Bonwit Teller – much too expensive! They had also written a poem for me. I realized that I was now their "other mother," something that touched me beyond words.

I had other wonderful experiences with my girls after they left the institution. With help from my colleagues, we were able to place all of them in jobs. At least 10 of the original 15 went on to become successes. A few years ago, I attended a reception held by a major airline. During the evening a woman, whom I'd noticed had been watching me intently, approached me, touched my arm, and guided me to a quiet spot. There she confided that she'd been in my class at the House of Good Shepherd. She was now in a managerial position at the airline. Of course, I was delighted to see her again.

It wasn't all perfection, though. I was deeply disappointed when one of my protégés, Mildred, whom we'd placed with American Express, disappeared from the office, taking several airline tickets with her. She had issued them for travel from Chicago to Los Angeles for herself and another person. She had also written another one and had convinced the airline to allow her to cash the ticket in, something one cannot do today. I was concerned that this would have such a negative effect on American Express, I asked Catholic Charities to cover the losses, which they did.

In 1978, I picked up my mail and found a letter with a return name and address that I didn't recognize. It was from Mildred. Inside was a check for $1,500 and a note that said how sorry she was for what she had done to me. It had taken her years to save up the money to repay her obligation. She had married and was raising two children. She worked for a doctor and lived in a nearby suburb. Mildred asked me to visit her, and I did. We had a joyous reunion. We sent the $1,500 check to Catholic Charities to repay them.

One Christmas Eve, Dave and I spent the entire evening down at the detention home for young delinquents, endeavoring to get a judge to allow us to take the younger brother of one of my girls home for the Christmas holiday. It was well past midnight when the judge, whom we'd located at home, finally agreed, as long as the boy stayed with us until he returned to the penal facility. Looking back,

I think it was incidents like this that made our program success-ful. We worked with these young women on a one-to-one basis and put in considerable time and energy on their behalf. They knew we would go all out for them, for any legitimate purpose. That knowl-edge as well as slowly growing trust kept them with us through the program. There were so many times in their rehabilitation when we could have lost them.

I spent a good deal of time at the detention home with Margo. She was incredible and certainly one of the most devoted social workers I had ever met in my entire career. She and the girls had great rapport and I'm sure she was responsible for the rehabilitation of many who came through the House of Good Shepherd program. Margo was the one who went through the process of choosing candidates for the institution. I remember going up to the dismal quarters where these young offenders were housed and finding, to my horror, that abused babies and small children were also being held there until social workers could find foster homes for them. I cannot begin to describe how pitiful these little ones were. They would hang on me, crying desperately and begging me not to leave. It broke my heart. I knew then that I had to get involved in fighting for better condi-tions for these innocent victims. We finally succeeded, but as usual in dealing with bureaucracy, it took some battling.

After two years, Mother Helene left the House of Good Shepherd, and for some inexplicable reason, our program was cancelled. I was extremely upset by this decision, especially when I found that the girls were taking ballet lessons in the time slot our course had occupied. Another Roman Catholic orphanage, Angel Guardian, approached me and asked if I would be interested in conducting the course on their premises, since they had a good number of teen-agers who might benefit from the experience. We introduced the course and continued to teach it for several years until the orphan-age closed. Again, we turned out highly qualified young people who were able to find jobs in our industry as soon as they were 18 and on their own.

LESSONS LEARNED

———

Cast thy bread upon the water.
Oh yes, the day I volunteered to teach a travel program
in a girls' reformatory proved to be one of the great lessons
of my life. These unfortunate teen-aged girls had already
experienced a lifetime of desperation. Many had been incarcerated
at a very early age and I was amazed when they actually responded
with great enthusiasm to studying and preparing themselves
for a future career in travel. They opened my eyes.
I learned that people who fall through the cracks can be redeemed.
This taught the importance of helping them along the way.
This volunteer program actually opened the door for me
to introduce the Echols International Travel and Hotel School.
It was incredibly successful for over 35 years.

———

CHAPTER 10

My New Entrepreneurial Adventure

In 1962, there still seemed to be great interest in the travel courses I was running. At that time, although there were excellent travel schools throughout Europe, there were none in the United States. Since I thoroughly enjoyed this industry, I asked David to place an ad to determine if there was true interest in such a course.

The response we received was overwhelming. So now here I was, with a group of people who were anxious to attend a travel school operated by Evelyn Echols. I had enormous amount of work ahead of me. I needed to be ready to present the curriculum in a short amount of time.

My first call was to C.R. Smith, a friend of David's and Chairman of American Airlines. I described the program we had in mind and told him that we were certain it would succeed if professionals taught the courses. I was delighted with his reaction. American Airlines would help me write the curriculum and would teach the airline section for the program. I met with equal success when I visited Cunard Steamship Co., American Express Travel Services,

Holland American Cruise Co., and Pan American World Airways. Harvey Olsen, President of the famous travel agency in Chicago, also became one of my main supporters.

That was in early August. I flew back to Chicago, having no real promotional materials. But I managed to enroll 15 students for our first class, which started on September 23, 1962.

My concept of this course was that it must be taught by professionals who were currently in the industry. Therefore I was truly gratified when 15 major airlines, hotels, cruise companies, auto rental firms and tour operators all agreed to allow their staff to teach in my school. Obviously my concept was correct because for the next 35 years Echols International Travel and Hotel School was recognized within the industry as the best training program in the United States. At first I noticed that parents were reluctant to have their children enrolled in what they thought of as a trade school because there had always been a stigma to trade schools in this country. However, once they visited the school, they quickly endorsed the program. More and more young people who were disenchanted with the idea of going to college, were enrolling in the school. Then as word began to spread that we were operating with a 2% dropout rate and a 98% placement record, our courses were always completely full, year after year. Later on we sold two franchises to reputable graduates – one in Washington D.C. and the other in San Francisco. I spent a great deal of time getting them established and they, in turn, were wonderfully successful. The number one travel magazine, *Holiday*, ranked us as the number one travel school in America for almost 20 years.

Now I wanted to be sure that I also continued to help students in the inner city schools, so I began a scholarship program where we donated 100 scholarships a year to students who were recommended to us by the principals of inner city schools. We made it clear, however, in granting these scholarships, these students must actually prove to us that they were interested in a travel course and would abide by our strict rules and regulations. As a result, these young people, who for the first time in their lives were truly interested in education, became remarkably good students who were eligible for placement upon graduation.

I actually loved my new career. There was such satisfaction in seeing how much students appreciated the excellent training they were receiving. Our graduation attracted human resource representatives

One of the first classes at the Echols International Travel and Hotel School in Chicago.

from many of the industry's major corporations. Everyone wanted to be first in line to pick the most superior students.

Our Board of Directors consisted of the executives of many leading corporations. This too, of course, not only enhanced our reputation, but helped us enormously in improving the content and structure of our courses.

LESSONS LEARNED

Echols International Travel and Hotel School
became successful way beyond my hopes and dreams.
I attribute this success to the lessons I had learned
at the House of Good Shepherd. I made up my mind early on
that the teachers in my school would be the very best
and every student would be provided with such excellent training
that there was no doubt as to their being employable
upon graduation.

My charity work had taught me the importance of networking,
which I applied to our enrollment recruiting efforts.
It was becoming clear to me that each experience
was a building block for defining my life.

CHAPTER 11

Life Takes a Turn

In 1990, things began to take a very serious, negative turn in my life. First of all, David, my beloved husband, friend and mentor was notified by his doctors that he had an inoperable aneurism in the aorta artery and could die at any time.

David immediately assured me that he had no intention of dying, that doctors were not God and he would continue living to the fullest. In the 1970s he had introduced a brilliant course titled, "New Product Lab" at the graduate business school at the University of Chicago. He loved his involvement with students and continued to devote untold hours to the University. I, however, decided I could no longer spend the time I had been spending at the School if I wanted to be available when he was home for any reason or traveling on business. Therefore, I hired a gentleman to manage Echols International Travel and Hotel School and truthfully did not supervise him in the way that I should have. He had encouraged me to move the School to a more prestigious building and increase the square footage. This, of course, led to expensive décor for the office. Almost from the outset my employees, especially my most trusted accountant, Ron Tully, began to caution me about this man's capabilities. Because of my concern for David, I did not heed their warnings. At that time I had several very attractive offers to buy the School, but I felt I could not do this because when David died, I knew it would be very important for me to be busy and involved in the School which I loved so much. It had been our custom to spend David's birthday on August 29th and our anniversary on August 31st by taking a European trip. However, due to Dave's heavy schedule, for the next four years we spent this time in New York, rather than going overseas.

But on August 25, 1995, we broke the spell and took off for Wiesbaden, Germany. It was our 44th anniversary. I had chosen this destination because, although he did not complain, I noticed that David's energy level was diminishing and the Grandhotel Nassauer Hof had a wonderful spa, which I thought would be beneficial to him. The spectacular pool, located on the roof, is fed by mineral waters located directly under the hotel. This location is where Napoleon brought his troops for R&R. After spending hours in the pool, I noticed that David was able to walk much longer distances.

On the day of our anniversary, David ordered a delicious breakfast including a small bottle of champagne. After we ate, he went to the closet and took out a large white box that was beautifully decorated with a pink satin bow and placed it on the bed. He presented me with a handwritten message of love that brought me to tears. Our friend, Ann Landers, once said that she would give anything to have a man look at her the way David always looked at me. Now he, too, was crying and as we embraced one another, although we did not voice it, we knew this might be our last anniversary together.

My tears gave way to laughter when I opened his gift – a most glamorous French lace chemise and gown, in about a size 10. As I held it up, I said, "Darling, do you truly believe I could get into this?" He said he didn't know why not. I could not believe he still saw me in that light, especially since I now weighed 160 pounds.

Reluctantly, he agreed to take it back to the store and I shall always remember the look of incredible surprise on the saleslady's face when she saw the woman for whom this gentleman had made the purchase. I am sure she had assumed that some little cookie would be the recipient. As we selected an exquisite, yet more appropriately sized 14 gown, we all enjoyed a good laugh with the other clerks who had joined in the merriment. As we were leaving, we heard our saleslady say to her associates, "*War das wunderbar!*" – Wasn't that beautiful!

We were heading for a noon luncheon sail up the Rhine, so the saleslady arranged to deliver the package to our hotel. It was a gloriously sunny day, one I will always treasure. The boat was not crowded

Birthdays were important to us and David went all out when I turned 75. He threw a glorious party for me at the Drake Hotel in Chicago.

and as we enjoyed a lovely lunch with a delectable bottle of wine, we passed some of the world's most beautiful scenery. It was an awesome sight – centuries old castles, and miles and miles of picturesque vineyards, green forests and gorgeous flowers in every direction, as far as the eye could see. I only wish that everyone could experience an afternoon of Rhine sailing.

Exhilarated by our experience, we returned to the hotel, took a siesta, and then celebrated our anniversary in the exquisite and intimate dining room of the hotel. That night, as we retired, we agreed that this was indeed our best anniversary. Thank you, God!

After coming back to Chicago, David immediately returned to the University and set about making preparations for the forthcoming semester.

Saturday, September 9th, was a gloriously sunny and bright day in Chicago. We took McDougal, our sassy Yorkie, for a walk. We had driven up to Lincoln Park and then spent the next two hours strolling through the beautiful grounds, taking time to enjoy the fabulous flowerbeds and allowing Mac to chase the largest dogs he could find so that he could assert his authority – even though they could gobble him up in one bite. It always amazed us how Mac managed to frighten these animals, sending them scurrying for cover.

We stopped by the zoo to watch the ever-amusing porpoises and returned home happy and invigorated. I prepared lunch and Dave opened a good bottle of cabernet. All seemed to be in divine order on this delightful day. Little did we dream that this would be our last day together on earth. David watched the Notre Dame football game and then said he was going to take a nap. I was in the kitchen when I heard him call me. I went into the bedroom and before he even spoke I knew the inevitable had happened. He was ashen and was having difficulty standing. He apparently was trying to get to the bathroom. He spoke quietly, "Darling, I'm sorry to be leaving you. The artery had ruptured."

Dave had lived a full, happy, fulfilling life over the past five years, but now it was over. Thinking back, I believe I did exactly what we agreed would be done on this fatal day.

He laid down on the bed and as I held him, I called 911. We had agreed that we would get him to the hospital but under no circumstances would the doctors torture him needlessly by endeavoring to save his life. They would immediately administer morphine intravenously. While we waited for the medics to arrive, we talked about the 44 years of the incredibly beautiful life we shared. This was a love story that very few are ever fortunate enough to experience. Some believe it never happens. Believe me, it does. We lived for one another and thereby made one another totally happy through good times and bad. As his voice became weaker, he said that the very happiest days of his life were the times we were alone together.

The ambulance arrived and as we were admitted to the emergency room, it was fortunate that I had not only his living will, but also his power of attorney. They were determined to take David up for X-rays and since our doctor was out of town, I stood alone in my determination that they would not allow him to suffer through meaningless procedures, but would immediately begin morphine injections and leave us alone. My assertive threat of a lawsuit finally convinced everyone to do as I wished.

Our good friend, Father McLaughlin, pastor of Holy Name Cathedral, arrived and prayed with David and administered Last Rites. He also gave me wonderful words of encouragement. After Father departed, we had probably another 30 minutes before David began to lapse into unconsciousness. At this point, he could not speak above a whisper, but he did manage to say, "You have been the most wonderful wife any man could ever hope for. I will give you three months to get back to life and this you must do. I'll be watching over you." In the last moment, he raised his head, looked directly at me, and barely whispered, "love." And then he was gone. As long as I live, those treasured moments will remain in my memory and give me great solace.

I found the medical staff to be extremely cold. I presume this is the way they are trained to be, but as most people I have spoken to agree, it is wrong. It is dehumanizing. One nurse did come in and ask if I wished to sit with David for a while. Why? He was gone. The gentle, handsome, brilliant, humorous, love of my life was no more. I simply wanted to get home, where I could be alone. Some very sympathetic volunteers took me to a cab and offered to accompany me home. However, despite the fact that I was numb with grief, I declined the offer. I spent the night praying and contemplating how my life had changed in the last several hours and pondering how I would address the many problems now facing me. How was I going to survive without David's constant care and concern? No more romantic interludes. No one to tell me how beautiful I was every day, even though I knew I was now well over 80 years old and no longer the well known model and TV personality he had married in 1951.

In the early morning hours, I gathered the strength to call our children, relatives, friends, and business associates. I spent the following days making funeral arrangements despite the fact that I was still functioning in a state of shock. The support and love of our children and close friends sustained me during this very sad period.

It is amazing how our Creator helps us through these times of crisis because certainly on my own, I was too numb to function. Hundreds of friends, students from David's classes at the University of Chicago, people he had helped throughout his generous life, all came to pay their respects. Then it was over. The children went home to California. Relatives had said their goodbyes and I was alone again. The Moody Institute radio broadcast "Music Through the Night" helped me get through the long hours when sleep was impossible. It was only after everyone had left me that I regained full consciousness. The funeral was held on a Tuesday. The very next morning I called the travel school to say I would return the following day.

LESSONS LEARNED

———

*These years presented the greatest challenges
I would ever experience and the many lessons learned
over the years definitely contributed to the fact that I was able to
weather these horrendous storms and came out scarred,
but victorious. I am very happy that I experienced difficult times
in my youth. If all had been easy up to this point, how would I have
known how to handle myself during this crisis?
Therefore, I say to you, dear reader, act positively
during critical times of your life. It will keep your future life
under control and enhance your potential for seeing
that rainbow around the corner.*

———

CHAPTER 12

God, Why are You Leaning on me So Heavily?

I knew if I were to retain my sanity, I would have to stay extremely busy. I asked that the staff not mention David's passing since I could not talk about it. Students, teachers, and staff all greeted me, showing their deep concern with kind gestures, making it possible for me to get back to work.

What a blessing it was to be busy, having problems to solve and decisions to make for ten hours per day! What work would I have done otherwise?

Friends insisted that I accept all social invitations, which was wise. My inclination was to get into bed and pull a pillow over my head. Thank God for my many loving friends.

Around this time, I was beginning to realize how serious the financial problems were at the School. My enrollment had fallen from 500 students a year to around 200. The School's expenses had also accelerated enormously – far outpacing income.

Both Ron Tully and my financial advisor and dear friend, John Meinert, urged me to close the School immediately before I incurred more debt. This I refused to do because I felt I could re-establish Echols International School to its former glory, attract the number of students I had in the past and over time, recapture our losses. I worked long hours and poured most of my resources into keeping the School going. I could not let my devoted staff and the many loyal companies that had supported me over the years suffer because of my mistaken judgment.

'Tis said that God does not give you more problems than you can bear. Well, He must have had a great deal of confidence in my ability to handle adversity from 1995 to 1998.

For some period of time, my staff had been telling me to call an ophthalmologist and set up an appointment for new glasses. I was having difficulty reading, so I finally complied. I walked over to the Kraff Eye Institute thinking what a burden it would be to wear glasses. Little did I know what awaited me. After an extensive examination, Dr. Lissner sat down next to me and said, "Evelyn, I have bad news for you. You have macular degeneration and are legally blind." Macular degeneration, what is that? Dr. Lissner assured me that macular degeneration affected only the frontal vision of your eye, but my peripheral vision was excellent in both eyes. This is what had made me capable of functioning up until now.

It seemed as though I was seeing everything through a heavy fog. I could no longer read any print less than one inch in size. I went with great trepidation to the Foundation for the Blind. The individuals there encouraged me greatly. Through them, I purchased a television set specifically equipped to magnify print. By placing reading material on a plate under the TV, I could then read the highly magnified print that appeared on the screen. What a Godsend!

Everyone recommended that I use a cane for fear that I would fall. This I flatly refused. I soon found that by keeping my head slightly turned I could make maximum use of my peripheral vision. I soon regained confidence, held my head up and maintained an erect posture. To date, my guardian angel has helped me to keep from falling into one of the many potholes I encounter on my almost daily one or two mile walks. I do have to be very careful when crossing streets so usually I wait until I determine that other pedestrians are proceeding. If no one is around and I can't read the signal, I listen to the sound of the car motors, which indicates when I would have the right of way, and say a little prayer before I step out into the street.

The necessity of working and enjoying what I do is a great advantage. Idle time is the time we are inclined to feel sorry for ourselves, so I am delighted to have very little time for indulgence.

When I finally decided that I must try to sell the School, it was too late. We were no longer the outstanding, successful school with an enviable reputation that many companies were interested in buying. Eventually in September 1997, I had to close the door. This, of course, was a heartbreaking experience – not only for me, but for my loyal staff who stayed with me to the bitter end.

LESSONS LEARNED

———

In all of the years of my life, this period was especially crucial.
How do you sustain yourself when your whole world falls apart?
I really can't say how I was able to handle those years,
but I feel that it was due to the lessons I learned,
especially during the Great Depression. I determined that
instead of looking back, I must constantly think of what
I was going to do in the future. It is amazing to me
how many positive opportunities began to come my way.
I began to realize that I was going to survive.

———

CHAPTER 13

A New Career Emerges
at Age 80

Now I had to face reality. My lawyer and my accountant met with me and pointed out the devastating news: I had lost five million dollars since 1990. Unless I wished to live a very frugal lifestyle, which I was not used to, I would have to go back to earning a living.

But who was going to be interested in hiring an 80-year-old, legally blind woman? I decided to ask this question of 20 CEOs who I thought might believe that I still had something to offer.

One of them was Paul Vallas, Superintendent of Schools for the City of Chicago. Happily, shortly after sending my letters of inquiry, I received a telephone call from Paul, asking that I meet him for lunch. We enjoyed a very long lunch together and he advised me that he was interested in offering the same type of training for high school seniors that had been available at Echols International School, so that they would be prepared for entry-level positions, especially in the hotel business, upon graduation. The salary he offered me was music to my ears and I told him I would be at work the following Monday. Within a month I had a full staff of teachers engaged and we began our first course.

Many of the students were sent to me by the incredible principals of schools on Chicago's Southside, as well as principals of other schools throughout the city. These public school students were quite different from the students who had attended classes at Echols International Travel and Hotel School, since they were college graduates or had some college experience. We were not sure that these young people would be motivated enough to devote the time and effort necessary to graduate from our course. Therefore, I decided that we would begin their training on American Airlines computers. I felt that the excitement they would experience by being able to connect to other parts of the world – for example, what was going on at Orly Airport in Paris, or what sporting events were happening in Rio – would whet their appetite for a career in this industry. This seemed to work wonders; 100% of the students immediately became involved.

Being trained by professionals in the industry made a big difference, too, but we had one big problem with the students – tardiness. So we decided to lock the doors at 9 o'clock and any student who was late had to go to the office. If they were late three times without a legitimate excuse, they would be expelled from the course. We also asked that they adhere to our dress code, so that when they were sent out on interviews, they would be used to dressing appropriately for business. If they could not afford new slacks, skirts or blouses, we made the purchase for them. American Airlines was extremely cooperative with us, in that they not only taught the course, but also hosted the graduation and allowed the children's parents to attend. The leading hotels and travel entities of the city showed up for our graduations and many of these students were hired immediately. I thoroughly enjoyed my two years with Paul and was sad when it came to an end. Paul went on to Philadelphia.

After my stint with Paul I was asked by Lois Weisberg, Chicago's Commissioner of Cultural Affairs, to put together a course for adults. This we did, but for one reason or another it was never extremely successful.

So here I was again, at age 85, looking for new opportunities to earn a buck. One avenue I wished to explore was writing. I immediately enrolled in a course in Creative Writing at Northwestern University. My professor was reluctant to accept me as a student. Number one, because of my age and number two, he wondered how I could possibly keep up with the material the students were reading in class. He finally agreed to accept me with the understanding that after a month, if I was not able to keep up, I would leave grace-fully. Fortunately during that month, he asked the students to write an essay of 1,000 words. With great trepidation I submitted my essay and received a note back that said, "You blew my mind," and so I was in. I graduated with a 3.7 GPA. After this, I decided to take another course in magazine writing and did equally well in that.

So now my friends were encouraging me to write a book, which I did – with devastating results. I had done five drafts of the book and the fifth draft I had taken to my good friend, my professor. He agreed it was a very good script. I brought it home and gave it to my relatively new secretary. I asked that she mail it to my publisher, which she did, but she mailed Draft #3, which still contained a sig-nificant number of errors. Because the publisher was not being paid to edit, they printed exactly what we sent to them. It was only after the book was already in circulation that I became aware of the problem. Therefore, although it sold a couple thousand copies, I was not happy about people buying it and we took it out of distribution shortly thereafter.

LESSONS LEARNED

———

Motivation is the key to success.
With a new career at the age of 80, I learned to keep on going
and keep on saying yes to life. It was very gratifying to find
that I could still make a contribution to the future
of our younger generation.

———

CHAPTER 14

Life Continues to Be
a Challenge

Fortunately for me, once again, several opportunities continued to present themselves. I think this came from the fact that I continued to work on various Boards and made a point to continue a policy I had always practiced, that of networking.

When anyone asked me if I would do something, even if I had no idea what I was getting involved in, I would say yes, and then find a way to do it. Jeremy Hills, who holds the Chair for Entrepreneurship at the University of Illinois in Chicago, had heard of me and elected me to the Entrepreneurial Hall of Fame at the University. From that a great number of opportunities emerged. I was asked to speak at one of Jerry's CEO conventions. This convention attracted students who were majoring in entrepreneurship from many universities – not only here in the Midwest, but from the East Coast, California and Puerto Rico. Jerry asked me to speak to these students, who numbered almost a thousand.

I did and as a result was invited to speak at universities around the country. I had no idea what my speaking fee should be, but gradually built it up to where it was quite lucrative. I continued to do this for several years. Unfortunately, although I have always received a standing ovation from an appreciative audience, the meeting planners seemed to be afraid to book me for fear that six or eight months hence I would no longer be around to fulfill my speaking engagement. So on to another new venture.

What's next? Joyce Gallagher, the Commissioner of the Department of Aging for the City of Chicago, contacted me and asked if I would like to do a television show for the City of Chicago. The format of the show was for me to interview senior citizens who were doing exceptional work in the field of volunteerism, since the city was endeavoring to encourage more senior citizens to become involved in this activity. This was a marvelous experience, because of the fact that so many of the volunteers had exceptionally interesting stories to tell. My guests on the show have ranged from 65 to 101 years of age and are devoting many hours to helping other people. One thing I noticed in interviewing these people is the fact that they are extremely happy to be so involved. There are so many opportunities of great interest in the world of volunteering. For example, the Art Institute and Museums, the Lyric Opera, the Chicago Symphony, schools, hospitals, neighborhood charities. It opens the door to new experiences, new friends and actually a new way of life for the senior citizen who has become a couch potato.

Now here I am, approaching 94, and I must say that I among the most blessed of people. Although I have a few aches and pains, I am still able to lead a very active business, civic, and social life. I attribute this to the fact that I have always been an incredibly optimistic person and can wait with great expectation for that rainbow which is just around the corner. I continue my work on Boards and am very involved in writing at this point. I do not know many 93-year-olds whose birthday would have been celebrated at a beautiful luncheon at the Woman's Athletic Club attended by 40 people, each of whom had paid $50 for the privilege of being at my birthday party. They also helped establish a scholarship fund at Dominican University, in my name.

One thing I know for sure is if an older person wishes to continue to be part of society, she must keep up her appearance. Fortunately I have a very extensive wardrobe, going back 40 years, which still makes it possible for me to look presentable. Then too, my yoga, which I learned in India over 40 years ago and continue to practice every day, contributes much to my agility and good health. I finally have come to the conclusion that if I am to stay well, I must be very careful about food. For that reason I now use only organic foods and definitely stay away from red meat, artificial sweeteners and chocolate. The chocolate has been the most difficult thing for me to give up.

My hope is that in my last years I will continue to be able to contribute to the welfare of mankind and when I can no longer do this, I pray that God will take me onto another venture in a hurry.

LESSON LEARNED

————

The lesson learned
is that it's been one great run!

————

CHAPTER 15

My Three Favorite Trips

Travel is always an exhilarating experience. One comes home from a trip with new memories that will probably never be experienced again.

When someone asked me recently about my wanderings around the world, what the three most memorable trips were for me, I can't say exactly why the trips I write about here were the most memorable, but I do know that when I am sitting quietly, reminiscing about my travels, these three experiences always come first. Our travels throughout the world greatly contributed to the happiness and concept of life that David and I shared. Although every trip added another dimension to our lives, Russia, India and Italy were very special.

The older I get, the more I appreciate the need for the interchange of people. If we are ever going to have world peace, it will only happen if we work at understanding, accepting and appreciating other cultures. What better way to learn these lessons than through world travel.

Dear Reader, I do hope that you will accept every opportunity that comes your way to get out and experience this wonderful, diverse, exciting planet on which we live.

RUSSIA

In 1961, David and I were invited to join the American Society of Travel Agents on a trip to Russia. We flew from Chicago to Frankfurt, Germany on Scandinavian Airlines. From there, we had the enviable experience of flying to Moscow on the Russian airline, Aeroflot.

The service on Aeroflot in the early '60s was quite different from American flights. The first problem was that the carpet was not attached to the floor of the cabin, causing me to trip on my way to the rest room. No food was served, and the disgruntled staff seemed totally unimpressed that, as travel agents, we could produce great numbers of tourists; or that members of the press who accompanied us would be writing about their travel experiences. On arrival at Moscow's airport, our luggage was scrutinized for a minimum of two hours. The agents seemed interested primarily in any books or magazines, which they confiscated.

By the time we arrived at the hotel and checked in, we had become a group of starving refugees. We dashed to the dining room only to encounter another great surprise. Because we were so late, the staff simply put large containers of boiled potatoes on the tables and had left. This was to be our dinner. Upon inquiry, we found there were no restaurants in the vicinity. How about candy bars or snacks? *Nyet.* We did find a few nuts in the bar and that was it. When we finally toddled off to bed, the sheets and blankets, needless to say, were not exactly what you would find in a Four Seasons Hotel.

Intourist, our official host, had notified us that we would be picked up and taken on a tour at 8:00 A.M. the next day. We were warned to travel only with the Intourist guide, but Dave suggested

David and I cherished our many travel experiences and what we learned from them.

it would be more fun if we took off on our own. So after the tourist buses departed, we walked a short distance to the railroad station and spent several hours watching commuters arrive. Some knew immediately that we were Americans and were most anxious to speak with us. Several made inquiries about how to get visas to come to the United States. While we were there, we also consumed a huge breakfast from street vendors – and survived.

We then decided to take a trip on the famous Russian subway, which was a wonderful experience. This was rather daring since we had no idea where we were going, but felt that if we only traveled a short distance, we would have no problem finding our way back to the hotel. We got to the station and could not believe how steep and endless the escalator seemed as we descended to the platform. To our surprise, we discovered that the train tunnels were extremely clean and decorated with beautiful murals. We traveled to the next station, disembarked, crossed to the other side and returned without difficulty. We felt we were being followed but couldn't be sure of this.

That night we were guests of the government at an official reception. Never before have I seen such enormous containers of caviar. The delicious delicacy was gobbled up unceremoniously, accompanied by wonderful large snifters of iced vodka. We were greeted by a good number of government officials, most of whom spoke perfect

English. I was dancing with a gentleman who kept trying to converse with me in Russian. A friend of mine, Carol Abrioux, danced by and said, "For God's sake, Evelyn, don't step on his toes. He's the head of the KGB." With this my dancing partner cracked up laughing, having understood every word she said. From then on, our conversation and our dancing were much livelier. He even tried to teach me some Russian folk dancing, and eventually he did admit that he was, indeed, the director of the KGB.

After another day of exploration, we attended the ballet, a glorious experience. We saw a magnificent performance of "Romeo and Juliet." I have always had a great respect for the Russian people because throughout their history, no mater how impoverished they were, they always supported the arts. Thanks to one of our traveling companions, who at the time was director of the Italian Tourist Office in Chicago, we had one glorious Italian meal after returning from the ballet. He had brought all of the ingredients to make pasta and invited us to supper at the Italian Embassy. No food ever tasted as good nor was as welcomed as this delicious meal.

We returned to the hotel rather late. After saying goodnight to everyone, David thought it would be fantastic to go out on our own and walk through the Kremlin. Despite the late hour, when we arrived, the Kremlin was brilliantly lit. Although there was not a sound or sign of any other person, we still thought we were being followed and hoped that our American passports would be honored if we were arrested. We spent at least two hours strolling around this majestic site, discussing its history and the fate of so many people who lived and worked here over the centuries. This turned out to be the most impressive part of our Moscow visit.

The following day, we went to Leningrad, now known again as St. Petersburg. Founded in 1703, the city still has the aura of a great imperial capital. As we walked along the Neva River, it was hard to imagine the horror the city had experienced during World War II, when it was under siege for 900 days and its citizens were dying from exposure and starvation. Our first impression of Leningrad was positive. All the people we encountered were extremely friendly. Many spoke English and seemed anxious to communicate with us as we passed them in the streets.

A day in the Hermitage was the highlight of our Leningrad experience. This would famous gallery was built in 1763 as a secluded retreat for Catherine the Great. She moved her art collection into the Hermitage, and over the next century and a half many more additions were made. Today, the Hermitage has 150 rooms filled with the world's greatest paintings and sculptures. For example, in one room alone, there are 27 Rembrandts. The four-room suite at the top level overlooking Palace Square is an incredibly beautiful setting and houses paintings by Renoir, Matisse, and Gauguin. The trouble with the Hermitage is that there is no climate control, and temperature fluctuations have led to tragic deterioration of many of the paintings.

After our two-day visit to Leningrad, we returned to Moscow before heading home. This trip left such an imprint in my memory that I now enjoy a much greater appreciation for Russian music, dance and art.

INDIA

"If India grabs you, you will never be the same," my dear friend, Norman Ross told me before my first trip to that country. India did grab me, and it has held on ever since, but it didn't start out that way.

My husband and I journeyed to India in the early 1970s. We arrived at the airport in Bombay in the early evening and as we drove to the Taj Hotel, we witnessed the squalor of the people who lived under the bridges. Every day, the bodies of people who had died the night before were picked up off the streets and piled into carts. Even today, in the early morning, Mother Teresa's nuns rescue some of these desperate people and care for them until they die.

By the time we reached the hotel, I was violently ill from our observations, as was David. Had we not been guests of the Indian Tourist Bureau, I sincerely believe we would have called the airline and booked flights home immediately.

What made the immense poverty around us all the more jarring was the drastic contrast with the other magnificent sights in Bombay: sacred cattle walking in the streets, snake charmers, elephants, old jalopies so overloaded with people they looked like circus acts, Rolls Royces carrying golden-robed maharajas and beautiful women in exotic saris entering the Taj Hotel. It didn't take long for us to discover the beauty and dignity of many impoverished people we encountered during our first few days in India.

The hotel had arranged for us to visit the temple of Mumba Devi, a goddess revered by the local Mahastian people. In 1996, Bombay was renamed Mumbai in honor of this goddess. We arrived at the temple in the early evening and I was immediately enthralled. We lit a candle and joined the procession leading to the shrine, where people would bow their heads and pray reverently for several minutes before depositing their candle on the altar. I thought of how different this was from the way we often jostle one another on our way to receive communion at churches in the United States.

In India, among Hindus, the caste system determines your social status and occupation. The caste system has four categories. *Brahmins* are the priests, scholars, and teachers; *ksatriyas* are the warriors and rulers; *vaisyas* are the professionals, merchants and artisans; and the *sudras* are the laborers and servants. About 15 percent of the Indian population, which is now over a billion, are know as the *untouchables* and are outside of the caste system. The only positions available for these unfortunate souls are the most undesirable jobs, such as cleaning toilets. Although the government supplies certain jobs for these individuals, they are greatly discriminated against. They are banned from many Hindu temples and aren't even allowed to draw water from certain wells. Many people believe that if they come in direct contacts with an *untouchable,* they will be contaminated and tainted. According to Hindu beliefs, these positions within the caste system are destiny, the result of karma. Their attitude is that individuals must accept their lot and not try to change how the cycle of life, death, and rebirth turns out. Therefore, many *untouchables* strive to make a living from begging.

We encountered some of these *untouchables* on our last day in Bombay. We invited the young concierge at our hotel, Josephina, who had taken such good care of us, to join us for lunch. Since the restaurant she recommended was only a block away from the hotel,

Dave suggested that we walk. Josephina was apprehensive about this because of the hundreds of beggars who would be pleading for money along the way. In the United States, we are used to violent street crime, but it is rare in India. Beggars don't carry guns or knives, and are never violent.

In the vast crowds surrounding us, we observed one young boy whose histrionics were incredible. His piercing eyes and beautiful expression were most captivating as he clasped his hands and pleaded with David. I wished I could have packed him up and brought him home with me, dirt and all. David asked Josephina if there was any way he could possibly donate to the boy's cause, but she said the others would probably attack the boy if David were to hand him anything. Just as we were about to reach the restaurant and the boy realized his efforts were going to go unrewarded, this street smart kid, whom we thought did not speak any English, suddenly yelled out, "Well then f*** you, mister!" At this, Dave and I laughed uproariously. Dave said, "I'm giving his kid some money, and I'll bet he's smart enough to get through this crowd intact." He was so smitten with this child that he cleaned out all the rupees in his pocket, the equivalent of $15, which our hero grabbed and stuffed in his pants pocket. He then sprinted off before anyone could possibly get a hold of him.

At the time, I was hosting a travel television show in the United States and Indian government officials had invited us to explore the country as their guests. We left Bombay and headed to Jaipur and New Delhi. As we traveled into the countryside, we came upon a group of six women, and although they were obviously impoverished, they were all beautifully clad in an array of homemade, brightly colored saris. Each carried a large jug of water on her head, maintained perfect posture and walked gracefully. They and others were washing their family laundry and laying it out in the sun to dry, making a carpet of wondrous color along the shores.

After spending a week going from Bombay to Jaipur and then to New Delhi, David and I were exhausted. I wasn't expecting it, but when we got to our hotel, I was about to face something I had never before experienced. Immediately after checking in, my old friend and famous New York designer, Bena Ramada, was there to greet us. She said I looked fatigued and needed some relaxation. She suggested I go to the hotel health spa for a yoga lesson. Bena introduced me to the yoga teacher, a beautiful 80-year-old woman named Madam Rabaldi. She took me by the hand and quietly spoke to me in her cultured Indian English accent and I felt that I was in the presence of an angel. For the next five days, she taught me the basics of yoga and maintaining inner balance. Since those five days with Madam Rabaldi over 35 years ago, my daily routine has started with a 30-minute yoga stretch period, which I think, in many ways contributes to my well being today. Thank you, Madam Rabaldi.

The second leg of our trip took us from New Delhi to Agra for a visit to the Taj Mahal. En route via automobile, we encountered throngs of people who were walking, riding in buses, on elephants, and in carts pulled by cattle. Luckily our driver spoke many different Indian languages and was able to glean that this mass of humanity was headed to see the Prime Minister, Indira Gandhi, who was visiting a new oil well facility. These joyful people, many of whom were walking distances of 20 to 30 miles in the broiling 100 degree sunlight, were waving excitedly and getting out of the way to make room for our car. I was amazed by their politeness and how quiet such a large crowd could be, which was later reported to be almost one million people,

Once we arrived at the location where Gandhi would be appearing, we stepped out of the car and our driver walked ahead of us. Then an incredible thing happened. The massive crowd, which had expended such enormous effort to get here, cleared a path for us. It was like Moses parting the Red Sea. We were very embarrassed by this since seeing the Prime Minister was much more important to them than it was to us. We refused to move forward. They insisted and we ended up right in front of Gandhi. A few times, I thought I would collapse from the intense heat, and I believe I only survived because of the low humidity. Mrs. Gandhi arrived about 20 minutes late and spoke for 45 minutes. Fortunately our driver had given me his chauffeur's hat and David was wearing a sun hat that he had purchased in New Delhi. As we were leaving, a good number of people in the audience spoke to us and wished us happiness and a full life.

We continued on to Agra and the next morning, thanks to the courtesy of the Indian Tourist Office, we were allowed entrance into the Taj Mahal at 7:00 A.M., three hours before it opened to the public. No experience in my life will ever compare to the time we spent alone in this monument of love.

The majesty of the incomparable Taj was nearly overwhelming.
We spent three hours there together and alone.

Shah Jahan was the father of 13 children, and built the Taj Mahal in memory of his beloved wife, Mumtaz Mahal, who died in 1631. Construction of the Taj required 20,000 workers and 18 years to complete. Since the sun was just beginning to rise over the Taj, we were able to see how the white marble, inlaid with precious jewels, changed colors and moods with each hour. I'm sorry that we were not also able to see it under the light of a full moon because I understand this, too, is a spectacular sight. At the sacred spot, where the tomb lies, I sat down on the floor, overwhelmed by beauty. Shah Jahan was later overthrown by his son and forced to live out the rest of his life jailed in a tower with a view of the Taj. His dreams of building a duplicate in black were left unfulfilled.

David and I wandered in different directions, both of us so completely absorbed in what we were seeing that there was no need to converse. I walked out on the grounds and looked down the Yamuna River where a man appeared, disrobed to his shorts and immersed himself up to his chest in this filthy water. There he stood facing east and saying his morning prayers for at least an hour. Ten o'clock arrived quickly, and David joined me out on the grounds where we sat quietly in reverence for our surroundings. As the gates opened and hundreds of people began to flood onto the premises, we said a prayer of thanks for the three hours we had spent in the presence of the most beautiful monument ever produced on this planet.

Our final destination on this adventurous trip was to Kashmir, reputed to be the garden spot of the world. However, getting there was an adventure unto itself. We boarded an Air India flight in New Delhi, and after waiting for a very long time, we were told to deplane because they had forgotten to fuel it. Happy were we that they discovered this slight error before taking off!

Later when we were airborne and beginning our flight over the Himalayas in a blinding snowstorm, David handed me a daily newspaper with a headline that read, "Air India pilots refuse to fly by instruments. They prefer to rely on their own instincts." The article went on to say that this had caused some accidents. What joyous news now that we were flying in a canyon where, when looking out the window, the gigantic white covered mountains on either side seemed to be scraping the wings of our plane! Fortunately, neither David nor I were afraid to fly, but I did notice quite a number of white knuckled passengers grabbing for their airsick bags.

For well over an hour, we continued flying over a scene of magnificent beauty. When the pilot finally said, 'We are coming in for a landing," the thought that he was not relying on technology made us somewhat apprehensive since it would be impossible for the crew to see the airport until we were practically on the ground. They set the plane down with a great aplomb, and as we were de-planing, Dave asked them to join us for a drink later, which they did. Yes, it was true. They had not made use of the instruments available to them, feeling that to do so would ruin their macho image.

We were taken by cab out to the lake where the houseboat we had rented for a week was anchored. The houseboats here were beautifully furnished with lovely antiques and wonderfully hand-woven rugs. There was color everywhere. Our manservant was an excellent cook and served us beautifully out on the deck. In the morning, while we were having our breakfast, vendors would arrive, offering their wares. They would paddle out in canoes loaded with a glorious array of flowers, especially pink lotus blossoms, which have religious significance in India. Others were selling jewelry, knickknacks, paintings, carpets, saris, hand-woven bags, and artwork of every description.

Needless to say, we purchased much more than we had ever expected to and fortunately, the Greek Counsel General in Chicago, our friend, Nico Macridis, had told us we could ship all our purchases to him, thereby avoiding customs and delays. Incidentally, he was very shocked to find weeks later that all of his offices were loaded with packages from India.

Watching the sun come up over the Himalayas in the morning and set in the west in the evening from this magnificent setting was an incredible event in our lives. We left there with a sense of peace. It is so sad that the ongoing war between Pakistan and India prevents others from having this wondrous experience nowadays.

We drove back through the countryside to New Delhi, boarded a plane, and flew home. As our plane circled over the Himalayas, I felt the grasp of India that my friend had referred to. I knew that my experiences of the past three weeks had left such an indelible impression on me that I was not the same person I was before the trip.

ITALY

Italy, especially Tuscany, has always been my favorite place on earth. David always said if we were going to Bermuda, I would somehow find a way to route us home by way of Rome.

One very special night, we came out of a nightclub at about midnight and discovered we were directly across from the Forum. It was a beautiful moonlit night and we decided rather than going directly to the hotel, we would take a leisurely walk through the famous ruins located between the Palatine and Capitoline Hills.

The Forum was now completely unoccupied, not a soul in the area. As we walked silently to the Curia, we visualized senators and famous orators pleading their cases, and Julius Caesar making his impassioned speech before he was assassinated. We spent two hours mesmerized by the history we were imagining and finally emerged through the Arch of Titus. David and I agreed over the years that this was one of our most awesome experiences.

Friends in Chicago had recommended a driver in Rome. The following day, Bruno took us on a tour of the Coliseum and other places of interest. He was a walking encyclopedia, not only of Rome, but also of the entire country. Of course, he took us to wonderful, intimate Italian restaurants where the pasta was incomparable.

The following morning, Bruno took us to the Vatican, but due to Pope John Paul's heavy schedule, a private audience could not be arranged for us. However, thanks to Bruno's many contacts, he was able to maneuver us through the crowd with the assistance of one of the Vatican priests. We were seated in the first row. The Pope left his study window and proceeded to walk around the entire square. It was obvious Bruno had connections because His Holiness came directly to us and spent two to three minutes talking to us. As he held our hands, we felt the presence of a truly holy man. We were

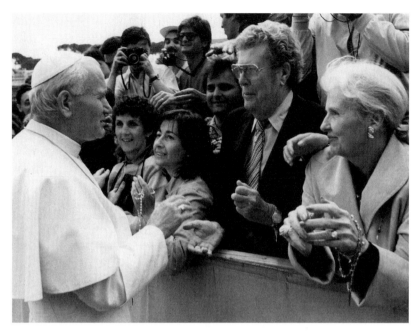

Bruno, our driver in Rome, was so well connected that he marched us right up to the front of the crowd so we could exchange a few words with His Holiness.

surprised when some beautiful pictures of the meeting were delivered to us at the hotel, compliments of the Vatican.

However, the truly incredible was yet to come. On the third day, when Bruno picked us up, he said he was taking us back to the Vatican. We could not understand as we had spent several hours touring the area after the Pope had completed Mass. En route we took on another passenger, an official from the Vatican. We drove through the back entrance of the Vatican, entered a building and ascended a series of stairs. Suddenly we realized we were in the Pope's private quarters. Bruno and his friend showed us the Pope's dressing area and opened all the closets to display his vestments and the cabinet in which he kept his gifts for special visitors. Bruno said, "What would you like to have?" Dave said, "We don't want a damn thing. Just get us out of here before the Pope walks in in his shorts!" Bruno assured us the Pope never got up until a certain time, but at David's insistence, we scampered out of these sacred quarters as quickly as we could. We could now understand why His Holiness, the previous day, had turned to Bruno as he was leaving us and queried, "Bruno, what am I going to do with you?"

Later, Bruno drove us through Tuscany and into Florence, my most favorite area in the entire world, and we enjoyed three days exploring the Tuscan Hills. One particular day we spent in Assisi, we were to celebrate Mass at the Basilica of St. Francis, but had arrived a little too early, so we stopped at a nearby confectionery and bought two huge ice cream cones of semifreddi chocolate plus a large box of incredible candy. We were sitting on a curb at 8:00 A.M., pigging out, much to the amusement if the natives. After a beautiful mass at the Basilica, we descended the stairs to where St. Francis is buried. There, a gentleman wearing a tuxedo came to us and said his daughter was to be married in the small chapel and he invited us to observe the wedding. It was a beautiful affair, with four splendid Italian tenors who sang the Mass. After the service, we were also invited to attend the reception, but felt we should be on our way to Florence.

Florence, to me, is the representation of the Garden of Eden. I love the ambiance, the architecture, the ancient sights, museums, music, people and unsurpassable food. Since I was still associated with the travel industry, we were guests of the Grand Hotel and they made their penthouse suite available to us. It has a terrace that overlooks the entire city of Florence and the Arno River. Naturally, we spent a good deal of time shopping and taking advantage of the beautiful arts, crafts, leather goods and silk scarves that are available in hundreds of shops throughout the city. We spent four days in this beautiful spot before proceeding to Venice.

We said goodbye to Bruno because David bravely decided he would drive the rest of the way. We rented a Fiat, which unfortunately broke down on one of the busiest highways in Italy. We were stalled, for what seemed like several hours, amid catcalls and insults from irate commuters. Several had tried to push us off to the side of the road but to no avail. Finally, a Fiat truck happened to be passing and saw our dilemma. We could not believe what was happening when the two mechanics lifted the entire front end of our car, shook it up and down several times, set it down, and away we went.

We arrived in Venice and were again hosted by the Gritti Palace Hotel, which is located on the canal. Here we spent a wondrous three days touring one of our favorite cities. We enjoyed many hours of operatic music and people watching in St. Mark's Square. On the last day, we took a motorboat out to the elegant Cipriani Hotel as guests of the manager, Mr. Resconi. As we were having lunch on the terrace on this gloriously sunny day, he asked us when we were planning to leave. We told him we would be leaving later in the afternoon for Milan but were sorry that the Orient Express did not board in Venice. He happily replied, "Oh, I don't know about that, we own the Orient Express." He immediately left the table to make reservations for us. What an impressive way to exit Italy! The trip was much too short, but we were extremely grateful for this accommodation. We arrived in Milan just in time to transfer to the airport for our trip back to the United States.

David and I cherished the memories of our many travel experiences and what we learned from them. These trips enriched the life we shared and helped us appreciate our last few years together all the more.

A noted lecturer once told me always to wear a hat when speaking because it gives the audience something to look at while you're warming up!

Approaching 94, Evelyn B. Echols continues to lead a very busy social and business life. She writes. She lectures. She serves on charity boards. She's still collecting awards from foreign governments for her work in promoting peace through travel. She dances. She travels. She swims and practices yoga. She knows that her very active days and spiritual guidance keep her sharp as a tack and gloriously happy.

www.evelynechols.com